# CAPM and CDL ....Prep
# [2 Books in 1]

*The Foolproof Guide with Tens of Question and Answers for Your Personal Management and Driver Certification (2021-22)*

**Copernico Cooper**

# CONTENTS

## CAPM Exam Certification Prep [Pmbok Guide 2021-22]

### PART I

### PART II Managing Cisco Routers

### PART III Authentication, Authorization, and Accounting (AAA)

# CDL Exam Certification Prep [2021-22]

# CAPM Exam Certification Prep [Pmbok Guide 2021-22]

*Go Above and Beyond. Boost Your Value in Personal Development. Start Your Career from Now! (limited edition)*

**Copernico Cooper**

# CONTENTS

## PART I

## PART II Managing Cisco Routers

## PART III Authentication, Authorization, and Accounting (AAA)

# ✚Introduction

## What is CAPM?

☐  CAPM represents Affirmed Partner in undertaking The board, an industry-perceived certificate for passage level task supervisors or venture chief wannabes. This accreditation test is directed by PMI, Task The board Establishment. You need to contemplate PMBOK most recent release (fifth, at the present time) to plan for this test.

➤ **Which implies that you can utilize any PMP arrangement asset for showing up for CAPM test too?**

☐  PMI's affirmation and certifications are set up by specialists so they are useful and significant. These are recognized by their worldwide turn of events and application, which implies that anybody across the globe can take this accreditation and apply the information to effectively oversee projects in any industry. PMBOK is a structure (and not a technique) with cycles of undertaking the executives cut and diced across Information Territories (Degree, Danger, Correspondence, etc.) and Interaction Gatherings (Starting, Arranging, etc.) making it pertinent across businesses. Notwithstanding, there might be project the executives devices or practices explicit to an industry that you may have to embrace as relevant.

☐  There are numerous shared characteristics among CAPM and PMP test, however for simplicity of utilization of data this post subtleties all that you require knowing for CAPM at one spot.

☐  This book is designed to help you prepare for the Cisco SECUR certification exam. The SECUR exam is the first in a series of five exams required for the Cisco Certified Security Professional (CCSP) certification. This exam focuses on the application of security principles with regard to Cisco IOS routers, switches, and virtual private network (VPN) devices.

☐  There are two rules you need to meet to show up for the CAPM test: 1. you need to have Auxiliary certificate (secondary school or same) or more 2. You need to have 1500hrs of expert venture the executives experience in a group OR 23 contact long periods of formal task the board instruction

- Any college degree in venture the board discipline or contact hour preparing from a PMI enlisted instruction supplier (REP) can be considered towards 23hrs of formal task the executives training. There are numerous different roads to get this schooling, for example,

☐ Schooling given by PMI parts

☐ Manager/organization supported preparing programs

☐ Courses via Preparing schools

☐ Online courses, as long as they permit you to take end obviously test and you pass it

> **How to apply for CAPM test?**

☐ You can either apply on the web or by sending paper based application to PMI. While online applications are handled in 24hrs, you need to hang tight for around 10 business days on the off chance that you send by post.

- Note that PMI suggests that you apply on the web.

☐ Note – you need to peruse and consent to PMI code of morals and expert direct (from the handbook accessible on PMI.org) prior to applying for the test.

> **Test Expenses**

☐ The most ideal route is to take up PMI participation and profit rebate on test expenses. This gets a good deal on acquisition of PMBOK control and some other venture the board books or assets too.

☐ Expecting you are a part and applying for online assessment you would be paying $225 (185 Euros).

☐ Download the handbook from PMI webpage to realize charge structure for whole blend of part/non- part, on the web/disconnected, assessment/reconsideration, etc.

☐ You can pay for test charges utilizing Visa, check, cash request or wire move to PMI.

☐ Note – PMI can discount your test charge in the event that you demand by composed methods at any rate 30 days preceding the test qualification termination date. You'll lose $100 handling expense in the event that you have not booked for the test as of now.

➢ **What is this Review cycle?**

☐ PMI arbitrarily chooses applications for review. In the event that your application is chosen you will get 90 days to submit following data:

1. Duplicates of formal schooling

2. Marks of your venture administrators/managers for the activities you have referenced on application

3. Duplicates of certificate for finishing of 23hr contact instruction

➢ **Re-certification?**

☐ Indeed. When you breeze through CAPM test, your affirmation will be legitimate for a time of 5 yrs. toward the finish of this you should re-confirm yourself to keep having a legitimate CAPM capability after your name. This re-confirmation should be finished during fifth year of approval period and not prior.

➢ **Test Content**

☐ CAPM test will have 150 inquiries, to be replied in 3 hrs. These inquiries are exclusively founded on most recent PMBOK (fifth version at the present time) control and are checked through psychometric examination.

☐ Nonetheless, not all inquiry goes towards evaluating your presentation. 15 inquiries out of these 150 will be 'pretest' questions. These are not considered for evaluating on the test and these are test inquiries to be remembered for the future assessment, in view of appraisal of how well they have been perceived and replied by understudies.

▪ Note – you can take break(s) during tests yet the clock won't be halted. So use breaks admirably, to crush tedium and get spirit once more.

☐ Here is the dispersion of test inquiries across PMBOK sections.

| PMBOK Chapter # | Chapter Name | % Questions |
|---|---|---|
| 3 | Project Management Processes | 15% |
| 4 | Project Integration Management | 12% |
| 5 | Project Scope Management | 11% |
| 6 | Project Time Management | 12% |
| 7 | Project Cost Management | 7% |
| 8 | Project Quality Management | 6% |
| 9 | Project Human Resource Management | 8% |
| 10 | Project Communications Management | 6% |
| 11 | Project Risk Management | 9% |
| 12 | Project Procurement Management | 7% |
| 13 | Project Stakeholder Management | 7% |
| | | 100% |

## CAPM Assessment Arrangements

☐ When your application is acknowledged, expense is acknowledged and review (if relevant) is sufficiently done, PMI will send you with PMI Qualification ID, assessment legitimacy period (which is one year) start and end dates and planning guidelines by email.

☐ Tests are conveyed by parametric focuses. You need to plan for the test at www.Prometric.com/pmi dependent on the data you got from PMI and dependent on accessibility of openings at the middle you wish to take the test.

☐ Upon the arrival of taking test

☐ You need to convey the accompanying to Parametric focus -

+ Government provided character card

+ You're most recent photo

☐ Show up at any rate 30 minutes early at Parametric focus. Sign in, show distinguishing proof and give the special Test ID that PMI sent you by email. You won't be permitted to take any things like number cruncher, food, sweater, books, and sacks and so on inside the test room.

➢ The accompanying things will be given by parametric staff – Number crunchers are incorporated into CBT (PC based test) test

- Scrap paper and pencils
- Erasable note sheets and markers

> **Test Results**

☐ Results are given following consummation of the test. Results are accounted. Pass/bomb score dependent on generally execution

☐ 3-point capability scale rating for every one of the sections: Capable, Respectably capable, Beneath capable

☐ Note – in view of the capability scale you can know your solid and feeble territories of PMBOK prospectus.

## The chapters of the book cover the following topics:

☐ Chapter 1, "Organization Security Fundamentals" – Part 1 is an outline of organization security by and large terms. This part characterizes the extent of organization security and talks about the fragile "difficult exercise" needed to guarantee that you satisfy the business need without bargaining the security of the association. Organization security is a persistent cycle that ought to be driven by a predefined hierarchical security strategy.

☐ Chapters 2, "Assault Dangers Characterized and Itemized" – Part 2 examines the potential organization weaknesses and assaults that represent a danger to the organization. This section furnishes you with a superior comprehension of the requirement for a successful organization security strategy.

☐ Chapter 3, "Safeguard Top to bottom" – Up to this point, an organization was viewed as secure on the off chance that it had a solid border protection. Organization assaults are getting considerably more unique and require a security pose that gives guard at numerous levels. Section 3 examines the ideas that coordinate all the security segments into a solitary, extremely successful security procedure.

☐ Chapter 4, "Essential Switch the executives" – this section subtleties the organization of the Cisco IOS switch and examines the IOS firewall include set. This section centers on the fundamentals undertakings that are needed to deal with an individual Cisco IOS switch.

☐ Chapter 5, "Secure Switch Organization"— this part discloses how to tie down the authoritative admittance to the Cisco IOS switch. It is essential to tie down this admittance to forestall unapproved changes to the switch.

☐ Chapter 6, "Validation"— this part examines the wide range of sorts of confirmation and the favorable circumstances and weaknesses of each kind.

☐ Chapter 7, "Verification, Approval, and Bookkeeping"— AAA has become a vital segment of any security strategy. AAA is utilized to confirm which clients are interfacing with a spe-cific asset, guarantee that they are approved to perform mentioned capacities, and track which activities were performed, by whom, and at what time. Section 7 talks about the combination of AAA administrations into a Cisco IOS climate and what AAA can essentially mean for the security stance of an organization.

☐ Chapter 8, "Arranging Span and TACACS+ on Cisco IOS Programming"— TACACS+ and Range are two key AAA advancements upheld by Cisco IOS Programming. Section 8 talks about the means for arranging TACACS+ and Range to speak with Cisco IOS switches.

☐ Chapter 9, "Cisco Secure Access Control Worker"— This part depicts the highlights and building segments of the Cisco Secure Access Control Worker.

☐ Chapter 10, "Organization of Cisco Secure Access Control Worker"— This section examines the establishment and arrangement of the Cisco Secure Access Control Worker on a Microsoft Windows 2000 Worker.

**Figure I-1** *Completing the Chapter Material*

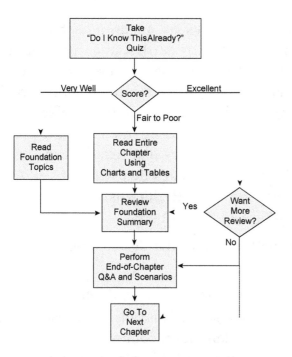

**CD-ROM-based** practice test, this book incorporates a Compact disc ROM containing a few intuitive practice tests. It is prescribed that you keep on testing your insight and test-taking abilities by utilizing these tests. You will find that your test-taking abilities will improve just by proceeded with openness to the test design. Remember that the likely scope of test questions is boundless. Consequently, your objective ought not to be to "know" each conceivable answer however to have an adequate comprehension of the topic that you can sort out the right answer with the data gave.

Explanation: The fitting reaction is 'stays as an argument against the property'. A repairman's lien is a particularly earth shattering commitment collection mechanical assembly that can be used by project laborers and workers that put in labor or materials to 'improve' authentic property. It is essentially a legitimate document that interfaces with veritable property and gives an ignored laborer for employ a security interest in the property. You ought to understand that a professional's lien reliably runs with the property. If a property is sold, the repairman's lien will not vanish. The argument stays against the property until the lien is totally satisfied. It doesn't have any effect who guarantees the property.

The errand of costs between the buyer and the dealer toward the end is called:

Explanation: The suitable reaction is 'customization'. Customization is the bit of money toward the finish of a property. This tally is consistently done by a land dealer, land salesperson, or land legal counselor. Eventually, this request should fill in as an update that all test-takers need to contribute the energy and effort to learn key land terms. Despite your express, in light of everything, you will run into explicit requests on your licensure test that present for implications of land industry phrasing.

A house sells for $195,000. The outright commission rate is 6%, of which the posting office gets 2.5% and the selling office 3.5%. Susan, the selling trained professional, gets a 60% piece of the commission. What sum will she secure as commission dollars?

Explanation: The proper reaction is '$4,095.00'. The preparation question is a fantastic delineation of such a figuring you might be drawn nearer to wrap up during your state's property allowing test. Here is the way you do it: Start with the total assessment of the arrangement. For the present circumstance, the house sold for $195.000. At that point, you need to know the hard and fast assessment of the commission got by the selling office. For the inspirations driving discovering this arrangement, we were unable to think often less about the posting office's reward. To move towards the last answer, take the certified arrangement regard and increment by percent of commission got by the relevant office ($195,000 copied by 0.035). The commission gained by the selling office is

$6,825. Susan gets 60% of this entirety. All things considered, she gets $6,825 copied by 60% (.60), or $4,095.

One of the activities you can take from this preparation question is that just one out of each odd number associated with the concise will be pertinent to finding the arrangement. In this model, the total commission (6 percent) and the posting office commission (2.5 percent) are essentially extra information; these numbers will not be used. Make an effort not to expect that each number ought to be associated with your calculation to discover to the right arrangement.

## This activity manual is unquestionably used

As an improvement to the substance in a fundamental land course, by one who has completed the land course and needs to overview while clutching take the state test, or by one not tried any traditional class anyway who needs to resuscitate principal authentic space considerations and thoughts.

Whatever the clarification Questions and Answers imitates the certifiable appraisal and enables you to advance toward the test with complete trust in your ability to pass.

Not all states use a comparative appraisal. The Relationship of Land Grant Law Specialists (ARELLO) invigorates all land regulatory workplaces to require guaranteed appraisals to test the competency of the up-and-comer. Confirmed test providers fuse AMP, PSI, and Pearson VUE.

## THE Point

This book involves distinctive choice inquiries and answers apportioned into subjects

Unsurprising with those subjects covered on most land approving assessments. Each major topic has subchapters and a movement of requests followed by illustrative answers. Additionally, there are addendums that cover standard state express allowing laws, math, review tests, and test last, most significant tests for salespersons and delegates.

## Quick Study GUIDE

If you end up with this book nearby and reasonably concise period in which to prepare, or in case you trust you are as of now masterminded, we suggest you first take the review tests and practice last appraisals in the back of the book. If you miss requests on a specific point, center your abundance examination time on those particular zones of the book.

We have furthermore included unequivocal quick study questions (allocated by the disguised box) that pass on the basic concentrations from each part. Complete these smart.

## Dealer QUESTIONS

For a quick expert review, certain vendor level requests are alloted with a bull's-eye in the edge. In any case, mediator contenders ought to regardless react to the aggregate of the requests in this book and not simply those set apart with a bull's-eye. Delegate tests cover comparable focuses as those found on an agent's evaluation and consolidate additional requests that oversee office affiliation, office the executives, and human resource headway.

### We should turn out a segment of such specialist questions and answers:

In the event that the expenses of an office, involving 24 full-time accomplices, are each year

$480,000, what is the work region cost? The plan is directed by isolating the amount of full-time accomplices (24) into the yearly expenses of $480,000. The proper reaction, by then, is $20,000.

What whole is remaining after all commissions, arrangements, and reference charges are paid out? The suitable reaction is association dollar.

In the event that a specialist expected to keep an essential separation from the possible loss of individual assets from a claim against the lender firm similarly as twofold assessment assortment, the BEST kind of business development would be:

a. Art S association.

b. Restricted association.

c. sole possession

d. general affiliation

The 100% commission blueprint is By and large priceless to whom? The proper reaction is an expert whose productivity is by and large high. Business applications may demand up-and-comers.

A. Age and race.

B. Religion.

C. Previous workplaces.

D. Companion's work.

The proper reaction is C. past workplaces. Moreover, shipper contenders should give interesting thought to Part D (Move of Property Ownership) and Part E (Land Lender).

## Directions to Use THIS BOOK

There are two strategies that you can use to enhance your sufficiency and energize study and learning. It is really a matter of individual tendency as for which approach is best for you.

One method looks like eating an elephant: take each eat thusly. Answer only five or then again six requests at the same time, and after each set of requests, investigate the fitting reactions by then do another set, and so forth this system will build your conviction as you come and give your brief info. Now and again, if you answer colossal quantities of requests at the same time without investigating the fitting reactions until later, you can't recall why you made the proper reaction choice you did.

The other strategy is to answer the entire test before looking at the suitable reactions, allowing one second for each question. Various people feel this not simply shapes scrutinizing speed yet moreover allows them to differentiate the rate right and the test objective (typically 70% to 75%) and definitely grows their trust in their testing capacities. Whichever system is used, mark your answers on an alternate piece of paper so when you need to restudy the material, you can't see the previous answers.

In addition, in case you save this paper, you can take a gander at the results the ensuing time around.

Exactly when you have ruled the whole of the parts and supplement material, don't hesitate to complete the preparation last appraisals. Hold adequate ceaseless freedom to take the last and review tests under reenacted testing conditions.

A Strategy FOR Analyzing

Sort out your examination time into two-to-four-hour pieces. Cover no more than four review parts at the same time. Long assessment gatherings are less productive. Sadly, basically scrutinizing the review material will not set you up for the test. To appear at a concentrated cognizance of the material, it is wise to chart your assessment material and make up in your cerebrum subject-related legitimate/sham requests.

**Introduction** Additionally, in the wake of scrutinizing, use the language words from each review part to make streak cards and subsequently use those cards to test you. In extension to using this book, in case you are in a relicensing class, structure an investigation pack with a couple of others.

The testing providers weight land lender, heavier than by far most of the various areas. Twofold your review time on association, postings, valuation of land, and arrangements. Entertainment Test- Taking Tips

- Find a quiet recognize (no phones or outside interferences) to venture through the tests in this book.

- Never leave a request clear. Restricted your choices and make an educated gather.

- Because you could outsmart yourself, don't look for misdirecting questions.

- In any case, picking the most fitting answer may anticipate that you should pay special mind to those answers that are simply mostly right.

If the request is scrutinized circumspectly, beginning presentations are overall right. As, a general rule, don't change an answer with the exception of in the event that you find later that it was misread or aside from if a future request "triggers" your memory.

In the wake of venturing through the tests in this book, check your results. Don't just survey those requests mistakenly answered, yet review each one

The Accreditation Test and This Arrangement Guide

The inquiries for every affirmation test are a firmly protected mystery. Truly on the off chance that you had the inquiries and could just finish the test, you would be in for a significant shame when you showed up at your first occupation that necessary these abilities. The fact of the matter is to know the material, not simply to effectively finish the test. We do understand what points you should know to effectively finish this test since they are distributed by Cisco. Coincidently, these are similar themes needed for you to be capable while designing Cisco IOS switches. It is likewise

**Introduction** vital to comprehend that this book is a "static" reference, while the course destinations are dynamic. Cisco can and changes the subjects covered on affirmation tests regularly. This test guide ought not be your possibly reference while getting ready for the affirmation test. There is an abundance of data accessible at Cisco.com that covers every theme in difficult detail. The objective of this book is to get ready you as well as could be expected for the SECUR test. A portion of this is finished by breaking a 500-page (normal) usage direct into a 20-page section that is simpler to process. In the event that you imagine that you need more point by point data on a particular subject, don't hesitate to surf. We have separated these themes into establishment points and covered every subject all through the book. Table I-1 records every establishment point alongside a short depiction.

Note that since security weaknesses and protection estimates proceed apace, Cisco Situation maintains whatever authority is needed to change the test goals without notice. Despite the fact that you may allude to the rundown of test targets recorded in Table I-1, consistently keep an eye on the Cisco Frameworks site to check the real rundown of destinations to be certain you are set up prior to taking a test. You can see the current test goals on any current Cisco confirmation test by visiting their site at Cisco.com, clicking Learning and Events>Career Affirmations and Ways. Note likewise that, if necessary, Cisco Press may post extra preliminary substance on the page related with this book at www.ciscopress.com/1587200724. It's a smart thought to check the half a month prior to taking your test to be certain that you have state-of-the-art content.

**Table I-1** *SECUR Foundation Topics and Descriptions*

| Reference Number | Exam Topic | Description |
|---|---|---|
| 1 | Secure Administrative Access for Cisco Routers | To ensure that your network is not compromised, it is important to ensure that administrative access to your devices is properly secured. There are several ways to ensure that administrative access to Cisco IOS routers is limited to only authorized administrators. The topic is discussed in Chapters 4, 5, and 11. |
| 2 | Describe the Components of a Basic AAA Implementation | A successful AAA implementation requires many components. The implementation of AAA is dis- cussed in Chapters 7 and 8. |
| Reference Number | Exam Topic | Description |
| 3 | Test the Perimeter Router AAA Implementation Using Applicable **debug** Commands | AAA implementation and troubleshooting are ex- plained in Chapters 7 and 8. |
| 4 | Describe the Features and Architecture of CSACS 3.0 for Windows | The Cisco Secure Access Control Server is discussed in Chapters 9 and 10. |
| 5 | Configure the Perimeter Router to Enable AAA Processes to Use a TACACS Remote | The implementation of AAA protocols (TACACS+ and RADIUS) are described in Chapters 7 and 8. |

| | | |
|---|---|---|
| | Service | |
| 6 | Disable Unused Router Services and Interfaces | The most effective way to secure the Cisco IOS router is to disable services and interfaces that are not necessary for the operation of the router. The correct steps for disabling the administrative interfaces are covered in Chapter 5. Disabling unnecessary services is discussed in Chapter 11. |
| 7 | Use Access Lists to Mitigate Common Router Security Threats | Access lists are a relatively simple way to filter malicious traffic. The different access list types and configuration steps for each are discussed in Chapter 12. |
| 8 | Define the Cisco IOS Firewall and CBAC | CBAC is the basis of the Cisco IOS firewall. Chap- ters 13 and 14 discuss CBAC in great detail and out- line the features of the IOS firewall feature set. |
| 9 | Configure CBAC | The configuration of CBAC is explained in Chapter 14. |
| 10 | Describe How Authentication Proxy Technology Works | Authentication proxy is a service that enables admin- istrators to proxy user authentication at the firewall. This IOS firewall feature is covered in Chapter 15. |
| 11 | Configure AAA on a Cisco IOS Firewall | There are many different aspects that all involve AAA. The configuration of AAA is discussed in Chapters 7, 8, and 9. |
| 12 | Name the Two Types of Signature Implementations Used by the Cisco IOS Firewall IDS | The Cisco IDS features on the Cisco IOS firewall are referenced in Chapter 16. |
| 13 | Initialize a Cisco IOS Firewall IDS Router | Configuration of the Cisco IOS router IDS is discussed in Chapter 16. |

| Reference Number | Exam Topic | Description |
|---|---|---|
| 14 | Configure a Cisco Router for IPSec Using Preshared Keys | VPNs using IPSec and Cisco IOS firewalls are discussed in Chapter 17. |
| 15 | Verify the IKE and IPSec Configuration | The steps required to verify the configuration of IKE and IPSec are referenced in Chapter 17. |
| 16 | Explain the issues Regarding Configuring IPSec Manually and Using RSA-Encrypted Nonces | The implementation of IPSec using RSA-encrypted nonces is discussed in Chapter 17. |
| 17 | Advanced IPSec VPNs Using Cisco Routers and CAs | Configuring VPNs using a certificate authority for peer authentication is a very scalable method for building multiple VPNs. This type of configuration is discussed in Chapter 18. |
| 18 | Describe the Easy VPN Server | The Easy VPN Server is defined in Chapter 19. The configuration steps for building VPNs using Easy VPN Server are also covered in this chapter. |
| 19 | Managing Enterprise VPN Routers | The products used to centrally manage an enterprise-level VPN using Cisco VPN routers are discussed in Chapter 20. |

☐ Overview of the Cisco Certification Process

☐ The organization security market is right now in a position where the interest for qualified architects immensely outperforms the inventory. Therefore, numerous designers consider relocating from directing/organizing over to arrange security. Recollect that "network security" is simply "security" applied to "networks." This seems like an undeniable idea; however it is really a vital one on the off chance that you are seeking after your security affirmation. You should be exceptionally acquainted with systems administration before you can start to apply the security ideas. Albeit a past Cisco confirmation isn't needed to start the Cisco security affirmation measure, it is a smart thought to in any event finish the CCNA certificate. The abilities needed to finish the CCNA will give you a strong establishment that you can venture into the organization security field.

☐ The security confirmation is called Cisco Guaranteed Security Proficient (CCSP) and comprises of the accompanying tests:

☐ CSVPN — Cisco Secure Virtual Private Organizations (642-511)

☐ CSPFA — Cisco Secure PIX Firewall Progressed (642-521)

☐ SECUR — Getting Cisco IOS Organizations (642-501)

☐ CSIDS — Cisco Secure Interruption Recognition Framework (642-531)

☐ CSI — Cisco SAFE Execution (642-541)

☐ The necessities for and clarification of the CCSP affirmation are illustrated at the Cisco Frameworks site. Go to Cisco.com, click Learning and Events>Career Affirmations and Ways.

➢ **Taking the SECUR Certification Exam**

➢ **Rules of the Road**

☐ We have consistently thought that it was befuddling when various locations are utilized in the models all through a specialized distribution. Therefore we will utilize the location space portrayed in Figure I-2 when doling out organization sections in this book. Note that the location space we have chosen is completely held space per RFC 1918. We comprehend that these locations are not routable across the Web and are not typically utilized on external interfaces. Indeed, even with the large numbers of IP tends to accessible on the Web; there is a slight possibility that we might have decided to utilize a location that the proprietor didn't need distributed in this book.

**Figure I-2** *Addressing for Examples*

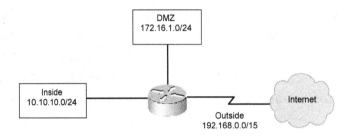

(or any public space)

It is our hope that this will assist you in understanding the examples and the syntax of the many commands required to configure and administer Cisco IOS routers.

Watchwords:

Appurtenance — An advantage or improvement having a spot with, and passing with, the land, For example, an easement appurtenance gives an advantage to one owner to use the other owner's property for passage and flight. Another model would be a home that has a bound garage. For assurance purposes, the separated garage would be seen as an appurtenant plan.

Store of rights—A belonging thought portraying every single one of those authentic rights that join to the obligation regarding property, including the alternative to sell, lease, burden, use, appreciate, preclude, will, etc business specialist—Someone who records and sells associations without the land. They work under rules spread out in the Uniform Business Code. Article 6 of the Code controls mass trades, the proposal of a business by and large, including trade devices, effects, and item. Resource Another name for singular property; resource fuses objects not con-prepared in the significance of real property. Singular property is moved by utilization of a bill of offer. Defeasible cost endowment—An affirmed space in which the grantee could lose his advantage upon the occasion or non-occasion of a foreordained event. There are two sorts of defeasible inheritances, those known as    a condition coming about, where the likelihood of reappearance occurs, and an ensured limitation, where the grantee's ownership subsequently gets done with the opportunity of returned (also called a charge essential positive). The words to the extent that, or while, or during are basic to making this second kind of defeasible estate. Devise—the enrichment of authentic property by will. The supplier is the terminated and the recipient is known as a devisee.

Emblements—creating harvests that are conveyed each year through work and industry, also called annuals or fructose industrials. At accumulate time, corn and soybeans would be examples of emblements, and, aside from if regardless agreed, possession would have a spot with the get-together who planted the collect.

Escheat—The reversal of private property to the public expert in circumstances where the decedent passes on without a will or without any recipients fit for obtaining, or when a property is abandoned. Charge clear—the greatest space one can have in certifiable property. A cost fundamental space is the most un-confined interest and the most complete and all out ownership in land: it is of questionable length, straightforwardly versatile, and inheritable.

Mechanical assembly—An article that was once up close and personal property anyway has been so joined to the land that it has become certified property (e.g., broilers, racks, plumb-ing). At whatever point set out to be an establishment, by then the article passes with the property regardless of the way that it isn't referred to in the   deed.

Intestate—to pass on without a genuine will. Not as much as freehold space—A home held by one who rents or leases property. This plan consolidates a permanent place to stay for a significant long time, an irregular residency, a space unreservedly, and a home at lenience. See Area 18 for a natty coarse explanation of such leasehold estates. Life area— any home in certified or individual property that is confined in term to the presence of its owner or the presence of some other appointed person. Lives homes may be made by will or deed, and determine what happens after the finish of the presence inhabitant's life estate. The property could get back to the main grantor or grantor's recipients (life home in reversal) or it could pass in extra part to an assigned remaining portion man (life estate in extra bit). Littoral rights—A landowner's case to usage of the stream coating their property similarly as the use of its shore zone. Littoral rights models consolidate ownership along huge streams like lakes or oceans. Riparian rights are water advantages of owners of land along moving streams, similar to safe streams and streams.

Probate—the formal lawful proceeding to exhibit or attest the authenticity of a will, The will is acquainted with the probate court, and leasers and interested standard ties are advised to acquaint their cases or with show since why the plans of the will should not be approved by the court.

Property—the rights or interests an individual has in the thing asserted; not, in the Particular sense, the genuine thing These rights consolidate the choice to have, to use, to block, to move, and to preclude, usually called the pile of rights.

Certifiable property—all land and appurtenances to land, including structures, structures, mechanical assemblies, divider, and improvements rose upon or affixed to the same, excepting, in any case, creating yields. Riparian rights—those rights and responsibilities that are unplanned to ownership of land coterminous or abutting on conductors, similar to streams and lakes.

Destinations—the financial and individual tendency for one territory of land over another

Loft—Rights in the land that pass with the development. In an easement by common perspective, the servient loft is resolved to allow the overall condo to use their region for passageway and flight, and moves the same obligation to any new buyer for the property. Essentially, the dominating condo gives his choice to continue when the prevalent loft's bundle is sold.

The Best Way to deal with Read for the Land Test

To transform into a real estate agent, you should complete your state's actual licensure test. A land test is by no means, a straightforward test. As a wellspring of viewpoint point, most of all applicants bomb the California land seller test on their first undertaking. Most various states have tantamount pass rates.

Do whatever it takes not to permit this information to stress you. There is inspiring information: You can pass. With fitting examination materials and the right method, you will be set up to float through your test with no difficulty by any stretch of the imagination. Here, our gathering offers the most flawlessly awesome assessment hacks to help you with setting up your territory test.

The Best Tips to Help You Study for the Land Test

## Use a Specialist Land Study Guide

While preparing for a land test, there is no convincing motivation to endeavor to sit around idly. It is immovably endorsed that you acquire induction to the best land prep study control. Land tests test a wide extent of different information, from industry-unequivocal language and complex plans to land law and land cash. There are entire courses that are told on all of these topics. All things considered, there is a monstrous proportion of relevant information open. You could analyze it forever.

This is the explanation it is extraordinary get capable land test study materials. Our examination guides take that gigantic area of information and decrease it down to the stuff that truly matters. We created our property test guides thinking about one target: Guarantee that our understudies breeze through the evaluation. There's nothing more to it. Whether or not you are gleaming new to land or you have been in the business for a serious long time, you can benefit by our examination guides. We offer a broad heap of models, test tests, and techniques to help you pass.

## Step through Preparing Tests

One of the keys to completing a land test is to take as numerous model tests as you can. Our assistants involve reams of legitimate land test questions. We by and large guarantee that the requests are suitably revived for the current rules, custom fitted to each state, and that they challenge our understudies so they know accurately what's in store during the genuine test. At the point when you start getting most of the preparation tends to right, you will understand that you are ready for test day.

Offer yourself a chance to Plan — Set Step by step and after quite a while after week Study Targets

As you begin perusing for the land test, it is a brilliant idea to set a fundamental course of action of attack. Ideally, you will not be constrained to pack the whole of the information at last. With a lot of workable step by step and after quite a while after week targets, you can persistently set yourself up for the test. This raises a critical issue: How long does it need to peruse for the land test?

There is no one right reaction to this request. Be that as it may, best test-takers spend some place in the scope of 60 and 90 days getting ready for the test. Clearly, this shouldn't suggest that that you are totally stuck between a rock and a hard place if you are endeavoring to pack at last. In case you are as of now spending all accessible time, you need the most perfect land concentrate direct: pick your state and start now.

## Review Test-Taking Methods

Finally, when test day moves close, it is a brilliant idea to overview some fundamental test-taking methods. On the edges, acknowledging how to feasibly take a different choice test can help with having a veritable impact. For example, one of the significant frameworks that we recommend is dealing with the hard requests by clearing out the fitting reactions that you know isn't right. Another strategy is to gotten back to questions that are entrapping you and locate all the basic arrangements down first. Past knowing the information — which is undeniably the primary piece of completing a land test — extraordinary evaluation taking affinities can be valuable.

## Get Second Permission to the Best Land Test Study Materials

A considerable number understudies have used our advantageous examination associates and free land tests to complete their test on their first endeavor. We are certain that our structure we work for — so much that we offer a full, no requests presented to genuine guarantee. You will complete the test, or we will offer you an all-out markdown. Is it precise to say that you are set up to begin preparing for your state's test? There could be not any more incredible time than today.

# CHAPTER 1
# Network Security Essentials

The term network security characterizes a wide scope of complex subjects. To comprehend the individual subjects and how they identify with one another, it is significant for you to initially take a gander at the 10,000 foot view and get a comprehension of the significance of the whole idea. Wonder why you lock the way to your home. The appropriate response is likely that you don't need somebody to stroll in and take your stuff. You can consider network security in much a similar design. Security is applied to your organization to forestall unapproved interruptions and robbery or harm of property. For this situation the "property" is "information." In this data age, information has become a truly significant product with both public and private associations making the security of their resources a high need.

**Table 1-1** *"Do I Know This Already?" Foundation Topics Section-to-Question Mapping*

| Foundation Topics Section | Questions Covered in This Section |
| --- | --- |
| Definition of Network Security | 11 |
| Balancing the Business Need with the Security Requirement | 9 |
| Security Policies | 1, 2, 3, 5, 6, 7, 10 |
| Network Security as a Process | 4 |
| Network Security as a Legal Issue | 8 |

**CAUTION** The objective of self-evaluation is to check your dominance of the subjects in this section. On the off chance that you don't have the foggiest idea about the response to an inquiry or are just part of the way certain about the appropriate response, you should check this inquiry wrong for reasons for the self-evaluation. Furnishing yourself credit for a response you effectively surmise slants your self-appraisal results and may furnish you with a misguided sensation that all is well and good.

1. Which of the accompanying ought to be remembered for the security strategy?

   a) Capabilities of the firewall

   b) Manufacturer of the firewall

   c) User obligations

   d) Sanctions for disregarding the arrangement

   e) A network chart

   f) Routing conventions utilized

2. Which of the accompanying workers ought to approach a duplicate of the security strategy?

3. Managers

4. Network engineers

5. Human assets

6. Temporary workers

7. All workers

8. Which of coming up next is valid about a security strategy?

   a. The strategy ought to require testing.

   b. The strategy ought not to be uncovered to the overall population.

   c. Cisco hardware ought to be indicated.

d. The strategy is a business report, not a specialized archive.

e. The strategy ought to be changed like clockwork.

9. Which of coming up next are acts coordinated by "the security wheel"?

a. Configuring

b. Securing

c. Implementation

d. Testing

e. Monitoring and reacting

10. Which of coming up next are advantages of a security strategy?

a. Leads to soundness of the organization

b. Allows the board to sidestep security endeavors

c. Allows the specialized group to have a limitless spending plan

d. Enables clients to know the results of their activities

e. Informs the client of how to break into frameworks

11. What are explanations behind executing a security strategy?

a. Enables the board to pass judgment on the adequacy of security endeavors

b. Enables the specialized group to comprehend their objectives

c. Enables clients to peruse the web unafraid of getting an infection

d. Enables the board to legitimize a bigger specialized group

e. Lessens costs because of organization vacation

7. True or Bogus: The security strategy is a record that is intended to permit the business to take part in certain electronic correspondences?

a. True

b. False

8. Choose the six primary objectives of security strategy:

a. Guides the specialized group in buying gear

b. Guides the specialized group in picking their gear

c. Guides the specialized group in arranging the gear

d. Gains the board endorsement for new staff

e. Defines the utilization of the best-accessible innovation

f. Defines the obligations regarding clients and managers

g. Defines sanctions for abusing the approaches

h. Provides a Cisco-focused way to deal with security

i. Defines reactions and accelerations to perceived dangers

9. What is the deciding component while assessing the business need against the security act?

a. Security is consistently the most significant.

b. The business need supersedes security.

c. You need to factor security with the Chime Security Model.

d. Security isn't significant except if your business is sufficiently large to sue.

e. None of the above mentioned.

10. What IETF RFC administers the Site Security Handbook?

a. RFC 1918

b. RFC 2196

c. RFC 1700

d. RFC 1500

11. True or Bogus: Organization security can be accomplished by having advisors introduce firewalls at your organization edge.

a. True

b. False

The answers to the "Do I Know This Already?" quiz are found in the appendix. The suggested choices for your next step are as follows:

**8 or less overall score,** Read the entire chapter. This includes the "Foundation Topics" and "Foundation Summary" sections and the

"Q&A" section.

- **9 or 10 overall score**, If you want more review on these topics, skip to the "Foundation Summary" section and then go to the "Q&A" section. Otherwise, move on to the next chapter.

# CHAPTER 2
# Attack Threats Defined and Detailed

This chapter discusses the potential network vulnerabilities and attacks that pose a threat to the network and provides you with a better understanding of the need for an effective network security policy.

## "Do I Know This Already?" Quiz

The purpose of the "Do I Know This Already?" quiz is to help you decide whether you really need to read the entire chapter. If you already intend to read the entire chapter, you do not necessarily need to answer these questions now.

The 10-question quiz, derived from the major sections in the "Foundation Topics" portion of the chapter, helps you determine how to spend your limited study time.

Table 2-1 outlines the major topics discussed in this chapter and the "Do I Know This Already?" quiz questions that correspond to those topics.

**Table 2-1** *"Do I Know This Already?" Foundation Topics Section-to-Question Mapping*

| Foundation Topics Section | Questions Covered in This Section |
|---|---|
| Vulnerabilities | 1, 5 |
| Threats | 10 |
| Intruder Motivation | 4, 6 |
| Types of Attacks | 2, 3, 7, 8, 9 |

---

**CAUTION** The goal of self-assessment is to gauge your mastery of the topics in this chapter. If you do not know the answer to a question or are only partially sure of the answer, you should mark this question wrong for purposes of the self-assessment. Giving yourself credit for an answer you correctly guess skews your self-assessment results and might provide you with a false sense of security.

---

1.  Your boss insists that it is fine to use his wife's name as his password, despite the fact that your security policy states that this is not a sufficient password. What weaknesses are revealed?

    a.  This shows a lack of an effective security policy (policy weakness).

    b.  This shows a technology weakness.

    c.  This shows a protocol weakness.

    d.  This shows a configuration weakness.

    e.  This shows that your boss is an idiot.

2.  You receive a call from a writer for a computer magazine. They are doing a survey of network security practices. What form of attack could this be?

    a.  Reconnaissance

    b.  Unauthorized access

    c.  Data manipulation

    d.  Denial of service

    e.  None of the above

3.  Walking past a programmer's desk, you see that he is using a network analyzer. What category of attack should you watch for?

    a.  Reconnaissance

    b.  Unauthorized access

    c.  Data manipulation

    d.  Denial of service

e. None of the above

4. Looking at the logs, you notice that your manager has erased some system files from your NT system. What is the most likely motivation for this?

   a. Intruding for political purposes

   b. Intruding for profit

   c. Intruding through lack of knowledge

   d. Intruding for fun and pride

   e. Intruding for revenge

5. Your new engineer, who has very little experience working in your corporate environment, has added a new VPN concentrator onto the network. You have been too busy with another project to oversee the installation. What weakness do you need to be aware of concerning his implementation of this device?

   a. Lack of effective policy

   b. Technology weakness

   c. Lack of user knowledge

   d. Operating system weakness

   e. Configuration weakness

6. Statistically, what is the most likely launch site for an attack against your network?

   a. From poor configurations on the firewall

   b. From the Internet over FTP

   c. From the Internet through e-mail

   d. From within your network

   e. None of the above

7. Your accountant claims that all the electronic funds transfers from the previous day were incorrect. What category of attack could this be caused by?

   a. Reconnaissance

   b. Unauthorized access

   c. Denial of service

   d. Data manipulation

   e. None of the above

8. Your logs reveal that someone has attempted to gain access as the administrator of a server. What category of attack could this be?

   a. Reconnaissance

   b. Unauthorized access

   c. Denial of service

   d. Data manipulation

   e. None of the above

9. Your firewall and IDS logs indicate that a host on the Internet scanned all of your public address space looking of connections to TCP port 25. What type of attack does this indicate?

   a. Reconnaissance attack, vertical scan

   b. Reconnaissance attack, block scan

   c. Reconnaissance attack, horizontal scan

   d. Reconnaissance attack, DNS scan

   e. Reconnaissance attack, SMTP scan

10. True or False: A "script kiddie" that is scanning the Internet for "targets of opportunity" represents a structured threat to an organization?

    a. True

    b. False

The answers to the "Do I Know This Already?" quiz are found in the appendix. The suggested choices for your next step are as follows:

✓ **8 or less overall score** – Read the entire chapter. This includes the "Foundation Topics" and "Foundation Summary" sections and the "Q&A" section.

✓ **9 or 10 overall score** – If you want more review on these topics, skip to the "Foundation Summary" section and then go to the "Q&A" section.

Otherwise, move on to the next chapter.

# CHAPTER 3

# Defense in Depth

As technology continues to advance, network perimeters are becoming very difficult to define. This chapter looks at the combination of security devices, policies, and procedures required to secure today's networks.

## "Do I Know This Already?" Quiz

The purpose of the "Do I Know This Already?" quiz is to help you decide whether you really need to read the entire chapter. If you already intend to read the entire chapter, you do not necessarily need to answer these questions now.

The eight-question quiz, derived from the major sections in the "Foundation Topics" portion of the chapter, helps you determine how to spend your limited study time.

Table 3-1 outlines the major topics discussed in this chapter and the "Do I Know This Already?" quiz questions that correspond to those topics.

**Table 3-1** *"Do I Know This Already?" Foundation Topics Section-to-Question Mapping*

| Foundation and Supplemental Topics Section | Questions Covered in This Section |
|---|---|
| Overview of Defense in Depth | 1–8 |

**CAUTION** The goal of self-assessment is to gauge your mastery of the topics in this chapter. If you do not know the answer to a question or are only partially sure of the answer, you should mark this question wrong for purposes of the self-assessment. Giving yourself credit for an answer you correctly guess skews your self-assessment results and might provide you with a false sense of security.

1. What is the major concern with having a compromised host on the internal network?

    a. It will make the security administrator look bad.

    b. Data on that host can be copied.

    c. Data on that host can be corrupted.

    d. The host can be used to launch attacks against other hosts on the network.

    e. None of the above.

2. What are some advantages in implementing AAA on the network? (Choose all that apply.)

    a. It limits access to only authorized users.

    b. It allows for single sign-on.

    c. It provides encrypted connections for user access.

    d. It restricts users to only authorized functions.

    e. All of the above.

3. Which devices can be used to segment a network? (Choose all that apply.)

    a. Firewalls

    b. Routers

    c. Switches

    d. Address scheme

    e. All of the above

4. Where does a host based IDS reside?

a. At the network layer

b. At the data link layer

c. At the presentation layer

d. As an add-on to the system processor

e. None of the above

5. What is the advantage of an anomaly based IDS?

a. They protect against unknown attacks.

b. They protect against known attacks.

c. They can restart a Windows server after a system crash.

d. They stop and restart services when needed.

e. They are very cost effective.

6. How does a signature based IDS determine whether it is under attack?

a. It compares the traffic to previous traffic.

b. It compares traffic to predefined signatures.

c. It correlates logs from numerous devices.

d. All of the above.

e. None of the above.

7. Why is it important to monitor system logs?

a. To determine the state of the network

b. To determine whether your systems are running properly

c. To pick a needle from the haystack

d. To determine whether you are under attack

e. To determine whether you can figure out what they mean

8. What is the advantage of using correlation and trending?

a. Most packages print out graphs that you can use for presentations.

b. They enable you to consolidate log data from multiple sources into a readable format.

c. They enable you to correlate log data from multiple sources to get a better understanding of the situation.

d. They enable you to delete traffic that does not apply to your network.

e. None of the above.

The answers to the "Do I Know This Already?" quiz are found in the appendix. The suggested choices for your next step are as follows:

- ✓ **6 or less overall score** — Read the entire chapter. This includes the "Foundation Topics" and "Foundation Summary" sections and the "Q&A" section.

- ✓ **7 or 8 overall score** — if you want more review on these topics skip to the "Foundation Summary" section and then go to the "Q&A" section. Otherwise, move on to the next chapter.

# CHAPTER 4
# Basic Router Management

☐ The Cisco IOS router and Cisco IOS firewall are actually the same hardware. The difference is a low-cost, advanced firewall feature set that was integrated into Cisco Internet Operating System (Cisco IOS). All the basic functionality of Cisco IOS Software remains on the IOS firewall with additional features added, called the firewall feature set. The Cisco IOS router is commonly referred to as the IOS firewall if any of the firewall feature set components are used. This chapter discusses access to and management of the Cisco IOS firewall.

☐ **"Do I Know This Already?" Quiz**

The purpose of the "Do I Know This Already?" quiz is to help you decide whether you really need to read the entire chapter. If you already intend to read the entire chapter, you do not necessarily need to answer these questions now.

The 10-question quiz, derived from the major sections in the "Foundation Topics" portion of the chapter, helps you determine how to spend your limited study time.

Table 4-1 outlines the major topics discussed in this chapter and the "Do I Know This Already?" quiz questions that correspond to those topics.

**Table 4-1** *"Do I Know This Already?" Foundation Topics Section-to-Question Mapping*

| Foundation Topics Section | Questions Covered in This Section |
|---|---|
| Router Configuration Modes | 1, 3, 4, 5–8 |
| Accessing the Cisco Router CLI | 9, 10 |
| IOS Firewall Features | 2 |

**CAUTION** The goal of self-assessment is to gauge your mastery of the topics in this chapter. If you do not know the answer to a question or are only partially sure of the answer, you should mark this question wrong for purposes of the self-assessment. Giving yourself credit for an answer you correctly guess skews your self-assessment results and might provide you with a false sense of security.

1.  What router configuration mode do you enter by default when connecting to a router?

    a.  Console

    b.  ROM monitor

    c.  User EXEC

    d.  Privileged EXEC

    e.  None of the above

2.  Which IOS firewall feature enables you to inspect traffic at multiple layers of the ISO model?

    a.  Multilayer inspection

    b.  Context-based access control

    c.  Tasteful inspection

    d.  Extended access control lists

    e.  Connection-based access control

3.  Which configuration mode is considered the path to the global configuration mode?

    a.  User EXEC

    b.  Line configuration

    c.  Interface configuration

    d.  Sub interface configuration

    e.  None of the above

4.  What configuration mode are you in when you see the following

prompt on Router A?

    a) User EXEC

    b) Global configuration

    c) Privileged EXEC

    d) Unable to determine because the prompt has been changed

    e) None of the above

5. What configuration mode must you be in to configure telnet access?

    a. Line configuration

    b. Interface configuration

    c. Telnet configuration

    d. Global configuration

    e. Connection configuration

    f. None of the above

6. What is the default symbol for the global configuration mode?

    a. hostname

    b. hostname

    c. router

    d. hostname

    e. hostname

7. What command do you use to exit the privileged EXEC mode?

    a) Ctrl-Z

    b) disable

    c) enable

    d) exit

    e) end

8. What are you most likely doing in the sub interface configuration mode?

    a. Changing the telnet password

b. Binding additional IP addresses to an interface

c. Changing the system password

d. Configuring system monitoring

e. Adding the default gateway

9. What access port would you use when connecting a modem?

a. Console port

b. Telnet port

c. Dialup port

d. Secure Shell

e. Auxiliary port

10. What clear-text protocol is not recommended for managing routers from external network segments?

a. Telnet

b. Secure Shell

c. RSH

d. SNMP

e. SMTP

The answers to the "Do I Know This Already?" quiz are found in the appendix. The suggested choices for your next step are as follows:

- **8 or less overall score** — Read the entire chapter. This includes the "Foundation Topics" and "Foundation Summary" sections and the "Q&A" section.

- **9 or 10 overall score** — If you want more review on these topics, skip to the "Foundation Summary" section and then go to the "Q&A" section. Otherwise, move on to the next chapter.

# CHAPTER 5
## Secure Router Administration

The Cisco IOS firewall helps secure the trusted network from unauthorized users. The security of the network also involves the security of the Cisco IOS firewall itself. In addition to physical security of the Cisco IOS firewall, it is important to secure administrative accesses to interfaces on the Cisco IOS firewall. This chapter discusses the different methods that are available in securing the administrative access to the Cisco IOS firewall.

### "Do I Know This Already?" Quiz

The purpose of the "Do I Know This Already?" quiz is to help you decide whether you really need to read the entire chapter. If you already intend to read the entire chapter, you do not necessarily need to answer these questions now.

The 10-question quiz, derived from the major sections in "Foundation Topics" section of the chapter, helps you determine how to spend your limited study time.

Table 5-1 outlines the major topics discussed in this chapter and the "Do I Know This Already?" quiz questions that correspond to those topics.

**Table 5-1** *"Do I Know This Already?" Foundation Topics Section-to-Question Mapping*

| Foundation Topics Section | Questions Covered in This Section |
|---|---|
| Secure Administrative Access for Cisco Routers | 1–10 |

**CAUTION** The goal of self-assessment is to gauge your mastery of the topics in this chapter. If you do not know the answer to a question or are only partially sure of the answer, you should mark this question wrong for purposes of the self-assessment. Giving yourself credit for an answer you correctly guess skews your self-assessment results and might provide you with a false sense of security.

1.  What are some of the steps that can be taken to secure the console interface on a router or switch device?

    a.  Administratively shut down the console interface.

    b.  Physically secure the device.

    c.  Apply an access list using the **access-class** command.

    d.  Configure a console password.

2.  How many characters can you have in an enable password?

a. 256

    b.  32

    c.  25

    d.  12

3.  Which of the following is the least restrictive privilege level?

    a.  0

    b.  22

    c.  15

    d.  17

4.  The **service password-encryption** command does which of the following?

    a.  Encrypts the configuration on the router

    b.  Stores passwords in an encrypted manner in the router configuration

    c.  Only encrypts the telnet password in the Cisco IOS configuration

**d.** Is only available on PIX Firewall

5. Which of the following commands are associated with privilege level 0?

   **a.** Disable

   **b.** configure terminal

   **c.** enable

   **d.** logout

6. Which of the following configurations displays a login banner when a router is accessed?

   *a.* Router# **banner exec** *d If you are not an authorized user disconnect immediately message d*

   *b.* Router **banner login** *d If you are not an authorized userdisconnect immediately d*

   *c.* Router **banner exec** *d If you are not an authorized user disconnect immediately d*

   *d.* Router **banner login** *d If you are not an authorized user disconnect immediately  d*

7. For maintaining confidentiality and integrity in accessing a router, ___is recommended over telnet.

   **a.** SSH

   **b.** AH

   **c.** Secure telnet

   **d.** VPN

8. How do you secure the Ethernet port on a switch? (Select two.)

   **a.** Disable unused ports.

   **b.** Configure port security.

   **c.** Set access list.

   **d.** Security cannot be configured on the port.

9. In the event of a security violation, what is the default response of the port?

a. Switches into restrictive mode

b. Switches into a temporary shutdown mode

c. Switches into permanent shutdown mode

d. Switches into a temporary restrictive mode

The answers to the "Do I Know This Already?" quiz are found in the appendix. The suggested choices for your next step are as follows:

- ✓ **8 or less overall score** — Read the entire chapter. This includes the "Foundation Topics" and "Foundation Summary" sections and the "Q&A" section.

- ✓ **9 or 10 overall score** — If you want more review on these topics, skip to the "Foundation Summary" section and then go to the "Q&A" section. Otherwise, move on to the next chapter.

# CHAPTER 6

## Authentication

☐ The identification and verification of users requesting access to a device or network is one of the core objectives of security. Although several methods of authentication are available, it is essential that one or a combination of authentication be used to secure the device or network. This chapter provides an introduction to the different types of authentication methods thatyou can use for Cisco devices and networks.

## ☐ "Do I Know This Already?" Quiz

The purpose of the "Do I Know This Already?" quiz is to help you decide whether you really need to read the entire chapter. If you already intend to read the entire chapter, you do not necessarily need to answer these questions now.

The eight-question quiz, derived from the major sections in "Foundation Topics" section of the chapter, helps you determine how to spend your limited study time.

Table 6-1 outlines the major topics discussed in this chapter and the "Do I Know This Already?" quiz questions that correspond to those topics.

**Table 6-1** *"Do I Know This Already?" Foundation Topics Section-to-Question Mapping*

| Foundation Topics Section | Questions Covered in This Section |
|---|---|
| TACACS | 5 |
| RADIUS | 7 |
| CHAP and PAP | 6, 8 |
| Configuring Line Authentication | 4 |

| Authentication | 1, 2, 3 |
|---|---|

---

**CAUTION**   The goal of self-assessment is to gauge your mastery of the topics in this chapter.   If you do not know the answer to a question or are only partially sure of the answer, you should mark this question wrong for purposes of the self-assessment. Giving yourself credit for an answer you correctly guess skews your self-assessment results and might provide you with a false sense of security.

---

1. Which of the following is true? (Choose two.)

    a. Authentication provides a method for verifying the identity of users.

    b. NAS cannot provide authentication.

    c. Usernames and passwords can be stored on NAS.

    d. Cisco does not support RADIUS.

2. Which of the following is the least secure method of authentication? (Choose two.)

    a. Username/password static

    b. Username/password aging

    c. Session key one-time password

    d. Token cards

3. Which of the following security protocols is not supported by Cisco network devices?

    a. TACACS+

    b. RADIUS

    c. Kerberos

    d. TLS

4. Which of the following command syntax is correct for creating a

---

username and password locally on the NAS?

    a. Router **username** maroon **password** k0nj0

    b. Router **username** maroon **password** k0nj0

    c. Router **set username** maroon **set password** k0nj0

    d. Router **set username** maroon **password** k0nj0

5. Which port is reserved for TACACS+?

    a. UDP 1645

    b. TCP 1645

    c. TCP 49

    d. UDP 49

6. Password Authentication Protocol (PAP)_____

    a. Involves a two-way handshake where the username and password are sent across the link in clear text.

    b. Sends username and passwords in encrypted format.

    c. Involves a one-way handshake.

    d. Is not supported by Cisco network devices.

7. Which of the following port does RADIUS use?

    a. UDP 49

    b. TCP 1645

    c. TCP 49

    d. UDP 1645

8. The CHAP authentication protocol _____

    a. Involves a three-way handshake.

    b. Involves a one-way handshake.

    c. Is not supported by Cisco network devices.

    d. Sends password in clear text.

The answers to the "Do I Know This Already?" quiz are found in the appendix. The suggested choices for your next step are as follows:

- **6 or less overall score** — Read the entire chapter. This includes the "Foundation Topics" and "Foundation Summary" sections and the "Q&A" section.

- **7 or 8 overall score** — If you want more review on these topics, skip to the "Foundation Summary" section and then go to the "Q&A" section. Otherwise, move on to the next chapter.

# CHAPTER 7

# Authentication, Authorization, and Accounting

An access control system has to be in place to manage and control access to network services and resources. Authentication, authorization, and accounting (AAA) network security services provide the primary framework through which you set up access control on your router or network access server (NAS).

## "Do I Know This Already?" Quiz

The purpose of the "Do I Know This Already?" quiz is to help you decide whether you really need to read the entire chapter. If you already intend to read the entire chapter, you do not necessarily need to answer these questions now.

The 10-question quiz, derived from the major sections in "Foundation Topics" section of the chapter, helps you determine how to spend your limited study time.

Table 7-1 outlines the major topics discussed in this chapter and the "Do I Know This Already?" quiz questions that correspond to those topics.

**Table 7-1** *"Do I Know This Already?" Foundation Topics Section-to-Question Mapping*

| Foundation Topics Section | Questions Covered in This Section |
|---|---|
| Configure AAA on Cisco IOS Firewall | 1–6, 9, 10 |
| Test the Perimeter Router AAA Implementation | 7, 8 |

| Using Applicable debug Commands | |
| --- | --- |

1.  Which of the following best describes AAA authentication?

    a.  Authentication is last defense against hackers.

    b.  Authentication can only work with firewalls.

    c.  Authentication is the way a user is identified prior to being allowed into the network.

    d.  Authentication is a way to manage what a user can do on a network.

    e.  Authentication is way to track what a user does once logged in.

2.  Which of the following best describes AAA authorization?

    a.  Authorization cannot work without accounting.

    b.  Authorization provides the means of tracking and recording user activity on the network.

    c.  Authorization is the way a user is identified.

    d.  Authorization determines which resources the user is permitted to access and what opera- tion the user is permitted to perform.

3.  Which of the following best describes AAA accounting?

    a.  Accounting is the way that users are identified before they log in to the network.

    b.  Accounting enables you to track the services users are accessing as well as the amount of network resources they are consuming.

    c.  Accounting cannot be used for billing.

d. Accounting is a way to curtail where users can go on a network access server.

e. AAA accounting is used only to track users logging on to the network.

4. Which of the following is the correct syntax to specify RADIUS as the default method for a user authentication during login?

a. Authentication radius login

b. login radius authentication

c. aaa login authentication group radius

d. aaa authentication login default group radius

e. radius authentication login

5. Which of the following authorization methods does AAA not support?

a. TACACS+

b. RADIUS

c. SQL

d. NDS

e. Cisco

6. What command enables you to troubleshoot and debug authentication problems?

a. Debug authentication

b. debug AAA authentication

c. authentication debug AAA

d. show authentication

e. show AAA authentication

7. How do you track user activity on your network access server?

a. You cannot track user activities on your NAS.

b. Use AAA authorization only.

c. Use AAA authentication only.

d. A and B.

e. Configure AAA accounting.

8. Which of the following commands requires authentication for dialup users via async or ISDN connections?

a. Authentication default radius

b. authentication default local

c. authentication line isdn

d. authentication login remote

e. authentication radius

9. After an authentication method has been defined, what is the next step to make AAA authentication work on the access server?

a. Set up AAA accounting.

b. Do nothing.

c. Apply the authentication method to the desired interface.

d. Reload the router or NAS.

The answers to the "Do I Know This Already?" quiz are found in the appendix. The suggested choices for your next step are as follows:

- ✓ **8 or less overall score** — Read the entire chapter. This includes the "Foundation Topics" and "Foundation Summary" sections and the "Q&A" section.

- ✓ **9 or 10 overall score** — if you want more review on these topics, skip to the "Foundation Summary" section and then go to the "Q&A" section. Otherwise, move on to the next chapter.

# CHAPTER 8
# Configuring RADIUS and TACACS+ on Cisco IOS Software

TACACS+ and RADIUS provide a way to centrally validate users attempting to gain access to a router or access server. This chapter discusses the basic configuration of a network access server (NAS) and router to work with TACACS+ and RADIUS servers.

"Do I Know This Already?" Quiz

The purpose of the "Do I Know This Already?" quiz is to help you decide whether you really need to read the entire chapter. If you already intend to read the entire chapter, you do not necessarily need to answer these questions now.

The eight-question quiz, derived from the major sections in the "Foundation Topics" portion of the chapter, helps you determine how to spend your limited study time.

Table 8-1 outlines the major topics discussed in this chapter and the "Do I Know This Already?" quiz questions that correspond to those topics.

**Table 8-1** *"Do I Know This Already?" Foundation Topics Section-to-Question Mapping*

| Foundation Topics Section | Questions Covered in This Section |
|---|---|
| Configure the Network Access Server to Enable AAA Processes to Use a TACACS Remote Service | 1–8 |

> **CAUTION** The goal of self-assessment is to gauge your mastery of the topics in this chapter. If you do not know the answer to a question or are only partially sure of the answer, you should mark this question wrong for purposes of the self-assessment. Giving yourself credit for an answer you correctly guess skews your self-assessment results and might provide you with a false sense of security.

1. Which of the following is the command to specify the TACACS+ server on the access server?

    a. Takas -server host

    b. takas host

    c. server takas+

    d. server host

2. Which is the default port that is reserved for TACACS?

    a. UDP 49

    b. TCP 49

    c. UDP 1046

    d. TCP 1046

3. Which of the following commands enables you to verify or troubleshoot a RADIUS configuration on a network access server?

    a. Show radius

    b. debug radius

    c. debug radius-server

    d. verify radius

4. What is the significance of the **takas-server key** command?

    a. It specifies an encryption key that will be used to encrypt all exchanges between the access server and the TACACS+ server.

    b. It is used to specify a special text when the user logs in to the access server.

c. It is an optional configuration and not required in the TACACS+ configuration.

d. It uniquely identifies the TACACS+ server.

5. Which of the following commands identifies a RADIUS server in a RADIUS configuration?

a. Radius-server host

b. radius-host

c. server radius+

d. server host

6. Which of the following are the basic steps that are required to configure RADIUS on Cisco IOS Software?

a. Enable AAA.

b. Create an access list.

c. Identify RADIUS server.

d. Define the method list using AAA authentication.

7. Which of the following commands deletes the RADIUS server with IP address 10.2.100.64 from a router configuration?

a. del radius-server host 10.2.100.64

b. remove radius-server host 10.2.100.64

c. no radius-server host 10.2.100.64

d. disable radius-server host 10.2.100.64

8. Which of the following is the default port used by RADIUS?

a. TCP 1685

b. UDP 1645

c. TCP 1645

d. UDP 1685

The answers to the "Do I Know This Already?" quiz are found in the appendix. The suggested choices for your next step are as follows:

- ✓ **6 or less overall score** — Read the entire chapter. This includes the "Foundation Topics" and "Foundation Summary" sections and the "Q&A" section.

- ✓ **7 or 8 overall score** — If you want more review on these topics, skip to the "Foundation Summary" section and then go to the "Q&A" section. Otherwise, move on to the next chapter.

# CHAPTER 9

## Cisco Secure Access Control Server

☐ Cisco Secure Access Control Server (Cisco Secure ACS) provides AAA services for dialup access, dial-out access, wireless, VLAN access, firewalls, VPN concentrators, administrative controls, and more. The list of external databases supported has also continued to grow, and the use of multiple databases, as well as multiple Cisco Secure ACSs, has become more common.

☐ This chapter describes the features and architectural components of the Cisco Secure ACS.

☐ **"Do I Know This Already?" Quiz**

☐ The purpose of the "Do I Know This Already?" quiz is to help you decide whether you really need to read the entire chapter. If you already intend to read the entire chapter, you do not necessarily need to answer these questions now.

☐ The 10-question quiz, derived from the major sections in "Foundation Topics" section of the chapter, helps you determine how to spend your limited study time.

☐ Table 9-1 outlines the major topics discussed in this chapter and the "Do I Know This Already?" quiz questions that correspond to those topics.

**Table 9-1** *"Do I Know This Already?" Foundation Topics Section-to-Question Mapping*

| Foundation Topics Section | Questions Covered in This Section |
|---|---|
| Describe the Features and Architecture of Cisco Secure ACS | 1–10 |

> **CAUTION** The goal of self-assessment is to gauge your mastery of the topics in this chapter. If you do not know the answer to a question or are only partially sure of the answer, you should mark this question wrong for purposes of the self-assessment. Giving yourself credit for an answer you correctly guess skews your self-assessment results and might provide you with a false sense of security.

1.  Which of the following devices are supported by Cisco Secure ACS?

    a. Cisco PIX firewall

    b. Cisco Network Access Servers (NAS)

    c. Cisco 412

    d. Cisco 550

2.  Which of the following is true about Cisco Secure ACS?

    a. Centralizes access control and accounting

    b. Centralizes configuration management for routers and switches

    c. Is a distributed security application only for firewalls

    d. Only supports Cisco products

3.  Which of the following user repository systems are supported by Cisco?

    a. Windows NT/2000 user database

    b. Generic LDAP

    c. Novell NetWare Directory Services (NDS)

    d. Cipher Tec database

4.  Which of the following password protocols is not supported by Cisco Secure ACS?

    a. EAP-CHAP

    b. EAP-TLS

    c. LEAP

d. ERTP

5. Which of the following is a feature of the Cisco Secure ACS authorization feature?

    a. Denying logins based on time of day and day of week

    b. Denying access based on operating system of the client

    c. Permitting access based on packet size

    d. Permitting access based on the type of encryption used

6. Which of the following are the types of accounting logs that can be generated by Cisco Secure ACS?

    a. Administrative accounting

    b. PAP accounting

    c. TACACS+ accounting

    d. RADIUS accounting

7. Which of the following is not part of the main services/modules that are installed for Cisco Secure ACS for Windows?

    a. CS Mon

    b. CS Admin

    c. CS Auth

    d. CSACS

8. What do the CS Mon services do?

    a. Provides logging services for both accounting and system activity

    b. Provides the HTML interface for administration

    c. Provides recording and notification of Cisco Secure ACS performance.

    d. Monitors firewall activities

9. Authentication and authorization function is handled by which service in the Cisco Secure ACS for Windows?

    a. CS Admin

    b. CS Authen

    c. CS Auth

    d. Secure Authen

10. Under which condition(s), using the Cisco Secure user database, are users forced to change their password?

    a. After a specified number of days

    b. After a specified number of logins

    c. The first time a new user logs in

    d. Never

The answers to the "Do I Know This Already?" quiz are found in the appendix. The suggested choices for your next step are as follows:

- ✓ **8 or less overall score** — Read the entire chapter. This includes the "Foundation Topics" and "Foundation Summary" sections and the "Q&A" section.

- ✓ **9 or 10 overall score** — If you want more review on these topics, skip to the "Foundation Summary" section and then go to the "Q&A" section. Otherwise, move on to the next chapter.

# CHAPTER **10**

## Administration of Cisco Secure Access Control Server

☐ AAA was conceived originally to provide a centralized point of control for user access via dialup services. As user databases grew, more capability was required of the AAA server. Regional, and then global, requirements became common.

☐ This chapter provides insight into the deployment process and presents a collection of factors that you should consider before deploying Cisco Secure Access Control Server (Cisco Secure ACS).

☐ "Do I Know This Already?" Quiz

☐ The purpose of the "Do I Know This Already?" quiz is to help you decide whether you really need to read the entire chapter. If you already intend to read the entire chapter, you do not necessarily need to answer these questions now.

☐ The five-question quiz, derived from the major sections in "Foundation Topics" section of the chapter, helps you determine how to spend your limited study time.

☐ Table 10-1 outlines the major topics discussed in this chapter and the "Do I Know This Already?" quiz questions that correspond to those topics.

**Table 10-1** *"Do I Know This Already?" Foundation Topics Section-to-Question Mapping*

| Foundation Topics Section | Questions Covered in This Section |
|---|---|
| Basic Deployment Factors for Cisco Secure ACS | 1, 2, 5 |

| Installing Cisco Secure ACS for Windows | 3, 4 |
|---|---|

**CAUTION** The goal of self-assessment is to gauge your mastery of the topics in this chapter. If you do not know the answer to a question or are only partially sure of the answer, you should mark this question wrong for purposes of the self-assessment. Giving yourself credit for an answer you correctly guess skews your self-assessment results and might provide you with a false sense of security.

1. Which of the following points do you have to consider before deploying Cisco Secure ACS?

   a. Dialup topology

   b. Number of users

   c. Remote access policy

   d. Number of Linux servers

2. Which of the following is the minimum CPU requirement for a Cisco Secure ACS server?

   a. At least a Pentium III 550 MHz

   b. At least Pentium II 330 MHZ

   c. Will work on any Pentium platform

   d. Both A and B

3. Which of the following are task buttons that are present on the web administrative interface of Cisco Secure ACS? How would network latency affect the deployment of Cisco Secure ACS?

   a. User Setup

   b. Group Setup

   c. Network Configuration

d. System Configuration

4. Which of the following are checklist items that come up during the installation of Cisco Secure ACS?

    a. Windows server can successfully ping AAAclients.

    b. End users can successfully connect to AAA clients.

    c. Your version is at least Netscape version 6.02.

    d. You have a T1 connection.

5. What is the minimum browser version that is supported by Cisco ACS version 3.2?

    a. Netscape 6.02 and Microsoft Internet Explorer 6.0

    b. Mosaic 3.0 and Microsoft Internet Explorer 5.5

    c. Netscape 7.0 and Microsoft Internet Explorer 6.0

    d. Mosaic 3.0 and Netscape 7.02

The answers to the "Do I Know This Already?" quiz are found in the appendix. The suggested choices for your next step are as follows:

- **3 or less overall score** — Read the entire chapter. This includes the "Foundation Topics" and "Foundation Summary" sections and the "Q&A" section.

- **4 or 5 overall score** — If you want more review on these topics, skip to the "Foundation Summary" section and then go to the "Q&A" section. Otherwise, move on to the next chapter.

# All Chapter Answers

## Chapter 1

1. a, c, d, e
2. e
3. a, d
4. b, d, e
5. a, d
6. a, b, e
7. True
8. b, c, e, f, g, i
9. e
10. b
11. False

## Chapter 2:

1. a, d
2. a
3. a
4. c
5. e
6. d
7. d
8. b
9. c
10. False

## Chapter 3

1. d
2. a, b
3. e
4. e
5. a
6. b
7. a, b
8. b, c

## Chapter 4

1. c
2. b
3. e
4. d
5. a
6. e
7. b
8. b
9. e
10. f

## Chapter 5

1. a, c, d
2. c
3. c
4. b
5. a
6. a, c, d
7. b
8. a
9. a, b
10. c

## Chapter 6

1. a, c
2. a, b
3. d
4. a
5. c
6. a
7. d
8. a

## Chapter 7

1. c
2. d
3. b
4. c
5. d
6. b
7. b
8. e
9. b
10. c

## Chapter 8

1. a
2. b
3. b
4. a
5. a
6. a, c, d
7. c
8. b

## Chapter 9

1. a
2. a
3. a, b, c
4. d
5. a
6. a, c, d
7. d
8. c
9. c
10. a, b, c

## Chapter 10

1. a, b, c
2. a
3. a, b, c, d
4. a, b
5. c

# ✛Conclusion

☐ The best strategy to complete the PSI Land Test; Fathom Your State's Test Content

☐ Since you will be taken a stab at your state's property laws and rules despite the more expansive subjects found on the public piece of the land test, you ought to comprehend what governs your state anticipates that you should be familiar with. This information can be found in up-and-comer information handbooks for each state, which are open for download on the PSI website (www.PSIexams.com).

☐ **Survey Course Materials**

☐ Numerous states have enlightening requirements that arranged delegates and arrangements experts ought to fulfill before getting able to sit for their approving tests. These can join on the web or grounds based land arrangements, cash and monetary issue courses offered by colleges and state-embraced land schools.

☐ Since these courses are requested by the state, putting aside exertion to review notes and course materials from your examinations - close by information associated with the up-and-comer information handbook - can help you with developing an assessment plan subject to material covered by the allowing tests.

☐ **Take a Preparation Test**

☐ Since PSI passes on the test, you may have to take in any event one practice tests that are directed by the PSI Learning Establishment. You can purchase these preparation tests one by one and take them absolutely on the web. After you complete the preparation test, you will get a score report that offers the correct reactions and an examination of your answer choices. Subsequently, you can use these tests to help perceive your characteristics and inadequacies for future examination.

☐ In resentment of the way that not supported by PSI, you can similarly find destinations that offer free practice questions or tests that can be used to test your general data and work on reacting to questions.

☐ **Investigate Open Assessment Resources**

☐ Test-prep resources are open from a couple of providers. A comparative school or land school you used to fulfill informational prerequisites may similarly offer test-prep courses for public and state fragments of your allowing test. You can moreover take a gander at a segment of oneself assessment resources spread out underneath to sort out which one is ideal for you.

☐ **PSI Getting ready Framework**

☐ PSI cooperates with untouchable planning providers, as 360 getting ready, to offer totally online land test-prep that is open for different states. You can take this planning exclusively and locate a consistent speed. Turning into an approved real estate agent incorporates something past acknowledging how to assist someone with finding a respectable home and having amazing capacities in arrangements. Getting ready to transform into a real estate professional incorporates homeroom hours and productive fulfillment of a test to test your knowledge, close by an application cycle to finally get the grant. The system that you choose to peruse for the land licensure and the express that you are living in will choose the schedule opening it takes for you to successfully complete your property licensure.

☐ States have their own necessities for the amount of hours needed for land planning. For example, Florida requires approximately 63 hours of study corridor coursework and around 45 hours of preparing after you get your grant. If you are in California, you will be expected to complete approximately 135 hours clearly work. Various states, similar to Pennsylvania, may even renounce the land coursework far and away if you hold a long term certificate in land or an associated degree. A couple of states require fundamental courses or school level courses to be done.

☐ **Land School**

☐ There are two choices to peruse when perusing for land licensure: on the web or homeroom. Length of study time and cost are two factors to consider while picking which elective best meets your necessities. With the regular homeroom course, you may want to complete the coursework in an ordinary of 4 to a half year. The time frame to complete the coursework will be directed by the state in which you live, as different states have a substitute number of hours required for coursework. Thusly, make sure to check warily what your state needs before you select and start the homeroom bundle.

☐ In the occasion that you choose to does you're inspecting on the web, you ought to pick guarantee online land school? This course could essentially contract your length of study time, especially if you are prodded and adjust quickly.

☐ **Land Test and Application**

☐ Each state has its own necessities for the Land licensure test and application measure. You ought to do a smidgen of investigation to find more about the specific costs for the test and the application in your state. A couple of states even license a short lived grant so you can begin working while you hold on for your position grant. Nevertheless, each state anticipates that you should find and work nearby a confirmed, approved Land vendor when you at first beginning filling in as a Real estate professional.

☐ **Turning into a Real estate agent Layout**

i. Generally talking, with commitment, focus, troublesome work, one should perhaps have the alternative to transform into a real estate professional inside a year. There are various components to consider with respect to the time slot it will take to transform into an approved real estate professional. Turning into an approved real estate professional incorporates something past acknowledging how to assist someone with finding a fair home and having amazing capacities in arrangements. Getting ready to transform into a real estate professional incorporates homeroom hours and successful satisfaction of a test to test your understanding, close by an application collaboration to finally get the license. The strategy that you choose to peruse for the land licensure and the express that you are living in will choose the schedule opening it takes for you to successfully complete your property licensure. In overview, here is what you should do to transform into a real estate professional:

ii. Examination all costs

iii. Pick a strategy for study

iv. Take and completed supported land courses

v. Effectively complete land test

vi. Apply for land license

vii. Locate an approved land mediator to mentor you

viii. Online Assessment for Transforming into a Real estate agent

☐ Study.com offers all you need to start toward transforming into a real estate agent. Courses give total consideration and substance is presented through associating with video activities and text works out. You can in like manner misuse online evaluations to watch your turn of events and get quick permission to dominate teachers through a request and answer feature. Sort out how you can start with Land Planning or explore the Land Test Prep course and study guide or take a gander at the Land Undertakings Manual for start.

☐ States have their own necessities for the amount of hours needed for land planning. For example, Florida needs around 63 hours of homeroom coursework and about 45 hours of tutoring after you get your license. If you are in California, you will be expected to complete around 135 hours clearly work. Various states, similar to Pennsylvania, may even defer the land coursework totally in case you hold a long term accreditation in land or an associated degree. A couple of states require fundamental courses or school level courses to be done.

☐ **Land School**

☐ There are two decisions to peruse when perusing for land licensure: on the web or study corridor. Length of study time and cost are two parts to consider while picking which elective best meets your prerequisites. With the standard homeroom course, you may expect to complete the coursework in an ordinary of 4 to a half year. The time frame to complete the coursework will be directed by the state in which you live, as different states have a substitute number of hours required for coursework. Thusly, make sure to check carefully what your state needs before you select and start the homeroom partition.

☐   On the remote possibility that you choose to do your considering on the web, you ought to pick guarantee online land school. This course could essentially truncate your length of study time, especially if you are prodded and adjust quickly.

☐   **Land Test and Application**

☐   Each state has its own necessities for the Land licensure test and application measure. You ought to do a touch of assessment to find more about the specific costs for the test and the application in your state. A couple of states even license a short grant so you can begin working while you keep things under control for your position grant. Regardless, each state anticipates that you should find and work nearby a guaranteed, approved Land expert when you at first beginning filling in as a Real estate professional.

☐   **Turning into a Real estate professional Blueprint**

☐   In general, with responsibility, focus, troublesome work, one should potentially have the alternative to transform into a real estate professional inside a year. There are various segments to consider concerning the interval of time it will take to transform into an approved real estate professional.

# CDL Exam Certification Prep [2021-22]

*The Most Frequently Questions and Answers Over the Past 5 Years to Earn Your Certificate on the First Attempt (limited edition)*

**Copernico Cooper**

# Contents

# How to Get a CDL?

To get a CDL, you should finish a state CDL assessment. While applying for a CDL, you should indicate whether you will be working in intrastate or highway business. In intrastate trade, you just drive your vehicle Inside a solitary state. In highway business, you may drive your vehicle across state lines just as cross into an outside country.

You should likewise give a Clinical Assessment Report (MER) and a Clinical Analyst's Authentication Structure (MEC) dated inside the most recent 2 years. You will be needed to give a MER and MEC at regular intervals. Clinical

assessments should be performed by a clinical inspector recorded on the Public Library of Guaranteed Clinical Inspectors.

When you have a CDL, you are needed to restore any non-CDL licenses back to the state. You can just at any point have one CDL, so in the event that you have a CDL from another state, you need to restore that also.

While going after a position, you should reveal all driving positions you have had in the most recent 10 years. You should inform your boss and the DMV inside 30 days of any petty criminal offense feelings (aside from stopping) paying little mind to the sort of vehicle you were driving when you got the infringement and notwithstanding the state you got the infringement in. You should likewise tell your manager inside 2 days if your permit was suspended, renounced, or dropped.

You or your manager might be fined on the off chance that you have more than one permit or you drive a business vehicle without a CDL or with a suspended, disavowed, or dropped CDL.

## CDL Preclusions

Your CDL might be suspended or disavowed on the off chance that you are sentenced for the offenses or on the other hand petty criminal offenses (while driving business or individual vehicles) recorded underneath.

Up and coming Danger

An "unavoidable danger" is the point at which you are at approaching danger of genuinely hurting yourself or the general population. The Government Engine Transporter Security

Affiliation may suspend your permit for all things considered 30 days (except if you've been informed of your privileges to a meeting) in the event that they trust you represent an "unavoidable danger". Lifetime Precluding Offenses

You will be given a lifetime suspension in the event that you utilize a vehicle to submit a crime that includes fabricating, circulating, or administering controlled

## substances. Significant Offenses

Your CDL will be quickly suspended for 1 year on the primary conviction (3 years if the offense happens while working a vehicle placarded for dangerous materials). On the subsequent conviction, you will get a lifetime

suspension (a few states will permit a reestablishment following 10 years). The following is a rundown of significant offenses.

Driving a commercial vehicle with blood alcohol level of 0.04 or greater

- (You will be put out of service for 24 hours if you have any amount of alcohol under 0.04)
  driving under the influence of alcohol or controlled substance

- refuse to take an alcohol test

- Leave the scene of an accident

- Use a vehicle to commit a crime

- Drive a commercial vehicle without a CDL or a revoked, suspended, or cancelled CDL

- Cause a fatality through negligent operation of a commercial vehicle Serious Traffic Violations

If you receive any 2 traffic violations (listed below) in 3 years, your CDL will be suspended for 60 days. If you receive any 3 traffic violations (listed below) in 3 years, your CDL will be suspended for 120 days.

Driving 15 mph or more over the speed limit

**Traffic Violations in Your Personal Vehicle**

Your CDL will be disqualified if you commit the following violations in your personal vehicle:

- Violations that involve drugs or alcohol

- Felonies that involve a motor vehicle

- Hit and Runs

If your license to drive a personal vehicle is suspended, revoked, or cancelled due to alcohol or controlled substance related violations or felony violations, your CDL will be suspended for 1 year. If you have second

conviction, your CDL will be suspended for life.

If your personal vehicle license is revoked, suspended, or cancelled, you will not be able to obtain a "hardship" license to drive a CMV.

Railroad-Highway Grade Crossing Violations

- If you violate any railroad-highway grade crossing law, your CDL will be suspended for 60 days on your first conviction. It will be suspended for 120 days on your second conviction and at least 1 year on your third conviction. Below is a list of Railroad-Highway Grade Crossing violations:

Drivers who are not always required to stop, failing to stop before reaching the crossing if the tracks are not clear

- Drivers who are not always required to stop, failing to slow down and check that the tracks are clear of an approaching train

- Drivers who are always required to stop, failing to stop before driving onto a crossing

- All drivers, failing to have sufficient space to drive completely through the crossing without stopping

- All drivers, failing to obey a traffic control device or the directions of an enforcement official at the crossing

### CDL Test and Supports

The CDL test is taken at your neighborhood DMV. It comprises of two sections: the Information test and the Abilities test. The Information test is a different decision composed test and the Abilities test comprises of 3 sections (vehicle investigation, essential control abilities, and street test). You should breeze through the Information assessments prior to taking the Abilities test. There are 8 Information tests:

- General Information (needed for everybody)

- Air powered brakes (needed to drive vehicles with compressed air brakes) • Six Support Tests

  ○ P: Traveler Transport (requires both Information and Abilities test

- o X: Tank Vehicle/Unsafe Materials Blend (needed to drive a blend or class A vehicle; requires an

Information test and the TSA Danger Evaluation)

- o H: Dangerous Material (needed to ship perilous materials; requires an Information test and the TSA Danger Evaluation) o N: Tank Vehicles (needed to ship fluids or gases in mass; requires an Information test)
- o T: Twofold/Triples Trailers (required if driving a vehicle that pulls twofold or triple trailers, requires an Information test)
- o S: School Transport (requires both Information and an Abilities test)

Everybody is needed to take the "General" Information test and relying upon the vehicle to be driven, might be needed to take extra Support tests as well as the Air powered brakes test. In the event that you bomb the Air powered brakes Information test or take the Abilities test utilizing a vehicle without compressed air brakes, your CDL will have a limitation mark that tells others that you can't drive vehicles with air brakes.

For the Dangerous Material underwriting, you will be needed to present your fingerprints and go through a personal investigation. You won't get a Perilous Material support if

- you are not a legal lasting occupant of the U.S. • you disavow your U.S. citizenship

- you have been indicted for specific crimes

- you have been mediated as a psychological imperfect or focused on a mental organization

U.S. Transportation Security Organization thinks of you as a security danger

## Driving Safely

As part of the "General" Knowledge test, you will be expected to know how to perform a vehicle inspection and drive safely. Vehicle Inspections

Federal and state laws require that you inspect your vehicle; federal and state inspectors may also inspect your vehicle. If a vehicle is deemed unsafe, it must be put "out-of-service" until issues are fixed.

A vehicle inspection should be done before, during, and after a trip. After the trip, day, or tour of duty, you should fill out a report listing any problems you found. During a trip, you should inspect the vehicle within the first 50 miles and then every 150 miles or 3 hours (whichever comes first). Watch the gauges for signs of trouble and look, listen, smell, and feel for signs of issues.

- Tires, wheels, and rims

- Brakes

- Lights and reflectors

- Brake and electrical connections to trailer

  Trailer coupling devices

- Cargo securement devices

Drivers of trucks and truck tractors transporting cargo must inspect the securement of the cargo within the first 50 miles of a trip and every 150 miles or every 3 hours (whichever comes first) after.

## ⊣ Check Steering System

- Check the steering system for the following problems:
- Missing nuts, bolts, cotter keys, or other parts
- Bent, loose, or broken parts, such as steering column, steering gear box, or tie rods.
- if power steering equipped, check hoses, pumps, and fluid level; and check for leaks

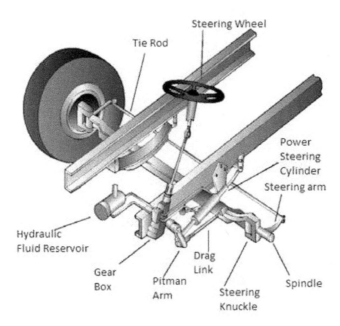

Steering wheel play of more than 10 degrees (approximately 2 inches movement at the rim of a 20-inch steering wheel) can make it hard to steer.

## ⊣ Steering System

- Check Suspension System
- Check the suspension system for the following problems:
- Spring hangers that allow movement of axle from proper position

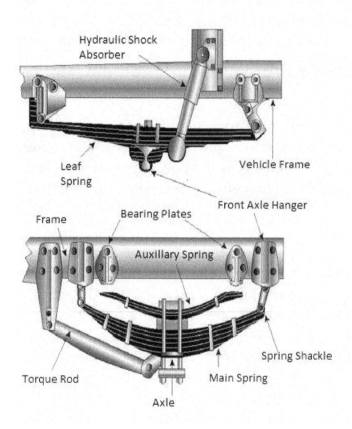

# Multi-Speed Rear Axles and Auxiliary Transmissions

Multi-speed rear axles and auxiliary transmissions are used on many vehicles to provide extra gears. You usually control them by a selector knob or switch on the gearshift lever of the main transmission.

## Automatic Transmissions

You can select a low range to get greater engine braking when going down grades. The lower ranges prevent the transmission from shifting up beyond the selected gear (unless the governor rpm is exceeded). It is very important to use this braking effect when going down grades.

## Retarders

Some vehicles have "retarders." Retarders help slow a vehicle, reducing the need for using your brakes. They reduce brake wear and give you another way to slow down. There are 4 basic types of retarders (exhaust, engine, hydraulic, and electric). All retarders can be turned on or off by the driver. When turned "on," retarders apply their braking power (to the drive wheels only) whenever you let up on the accelerator pedal all the way. Because these devices can be noisy, be sure you know where their use is permitted. Caution when your drive wheels have poor traction, the retarder may cause them to skid. Release the parking brake only when you have applied enough engine power to keep from rolling back. On a tractor-trailer equipped with a trailer brake hand valve, the hand valve can be applied to keep from rolling back. Speed up smoothly and gradually. Rough acceleration can cause mechanical damage. When pulling a trailer, rough acceleration can damage the coupling. When starting a bus on a level surface with good traction, there is often no need for the parking brake.

Speed up very gradually when traction is poor, as in rain or snow. If you use too much power, the drive wheels may spin. You could lose control. If the drive wheels begin to spin, take your foot off the

Importance of Looking Far Enough Ahead because stopping or changing lanes can take

a lot of distance, knowing what the traffic is doing on all sides of you is very important.

How far ahead to Look Most good drivers look at least 12 to 15 seconds ahead that means looking ahead the distance you will travel in 12 to 15 seconds. At lower speeds, that's about one block. At highway speeds it is about a quarter of a mile. Looking 12 to 15 seconds ahead does not mean not paying attention to things that are closer. Good drivers shift their attention back and forth, near and far. Look for Traffic.

Look for vehicles coming onto the highway, into your lane, or turning. Watch for brake lights from slowing vehicles. If a traffic light has been green for a long time it will probably change before you get there. Start slowing down and be ready to stop.

Road conditions Look for hills and curves- anything for which you will have to slow o change lanes. Pay attention to traffic signals and signs. Traffic signs may alert you to road conditions where you may have to change speed.

## Seeing to the Sides and Rear

Check your mirrors regularly. Check more often in special situations.

Mirror Adjustment. Mirror adjustment should be checked prior to the start of any trip and can only be checked accurately when the trailer(s) are straight. You should check and adjust each mirror to show some part of the vehicle. This will give you a reference point for judging the position of the other images. Traffic; Check your mirrors for vehicles on either side and in back of you. In an emergency, you may need to know whether you can make a quick lane change. Use your mirrors to spot overtaking vehicles. There are "blind spots" that your mirrors cannot show you. Check your mirrors regularly to know where other vehicles are around you, and to see if they move into your blind spots. Check Your Vehicle. Use the mirrors to keep an eye on your tires. It is one way to spot a tire fire. If you are carrying open cargo, you can use the mirrors to check. Look for loose straps, ropes, or chains. Watch for a flapping or ballooning tarp.

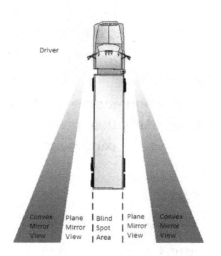

## Seeing Hazards:

What is a Hazard? A hazard is any road condition or other road user (driver, motorcyclist, bicyclist, and pedestrian) that is a possible danger.

Seeing Hazards Lets You Be Prepared. You will have more time to act if you see hazards before they become emergencies. You might make a lane change or slow down to prevent an accident if the car suddenly cuts in front of you. Seeing this hazard gives you time to check your mirrors and signal a lane change.

Hazardous Roads

## Move-Over Laws

The incidents of law enforcement officers, emergency medical services, fire department personnel and people working on the road being struck while performing duties at the roadside are increasing at a frightening pace. Move- over laws have been enacted, which require drivers to slow and change lanes when approaching a roadside incident to lessen the problem. Signs are posted on roadways in states that have such laws.

When approaching an authorized emergency vehicle stopped on the roadside or a work zone, you should proceed with caution by slowing and yielding the right-of-way by changing into a lane not next to that of the authorized emergency vehicle or work zone if safety and traffic conditions permit. If a lane change is unsafe, slow down and proceed with caution while maintaining a safe speed for traffic conditions. Slow down and be very careful if you see any of the following road hazards: Work Zones. When people are working on the road, it is a hazard. There may be narrower lanes, sharp turns, or uneven surfaces. Other drivers are often distracted and drive unsafely.

Workers and construction vehicles may get in the way. Drive slowly and carefully near work zones. Use your 4-way emergency flashers or brake lights to warn drivers behind you.

Drop Off. Sometimes the pavement drops off sharply near the edge of the road. Driving too near the edge can tilt your vehicle toward the side of the road. This can cause the top of your vehicle to hit roadside objects (signs, tree limbs). Also, it can be hard to steer as you cross the drop off, going off the road, or coming back on.

Foreign Objects Things that have fallen on the road can be hazards. They can be a danger to your tires and wheel rims. They can damage electrical and brake lines. They can be caught between dual tires and cause severe damage. Some obstacles that appear to be harmless can be very dangerous. For example, cardboard boxes may be empty, but they may also contain some solid or heavy material capable of causing damage. Off Ramps/On Ramps. Freeway and turnpike exits can be particularly dangerous for commercial vehicles. Off ramps and on ramps often have speed limit signs posted. Remember, these speeds may be safe for automobiles, but may not be safe for larger vehicles or heavily loaded vehicles. Exits that go downhill and turn at the same time can be especially dangerous. The downgrade makes it difficult to reduce speed. Braking and turning at the same time can be a dangerous practice. Make sure you are going slowly enough before you get on the curved part of an off ramp or on ramp.

## Drive-Wheel Skids

By far the most common skid is one in which the rear wheels lose traction through excessive braking or acceleration. Skids caused by acceleration usually happen on ice or snow. Taking your foot off the accelerator can easily stop them. (If it is very slippery, push the clutch in. Otherwise, the engine can keep the wheels from rolling freely and regaining traction.) Rear wheel braking skids occur when the rear drive wheels lock. Locked wheels have less traction than rolling wheels, the rear wheels usually slide sideways in an attempt to "catch up" with the front wheels. In a bus or straight truck, the vehicle will slide sideways in a "spin out." With vehicles towing trailers, a drive-wheel skid can let the trailer push the towing vehicle sideways, causing a sudden jackknife.

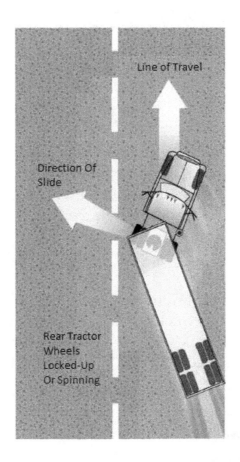

## Header Boards

Front-end header boards ("headache racks") protect you from your cargo in case of an accident or emergency stop. Make sure the front-end structure is in good condition. The front-end structure should block the forward

movement of any cargo you carry.

## Covering Cargo

There are 2 basic reasons for covering cargo:

- To protect people from spilled cargo.

- To protect the cargo from weather.

Spill protection is a safety requirement in many states. Be familiar with the laws in the states you drive in.

You should look at your cargo covers in the mirrors from time to time while driving. A flapping cover can tear loose, uncovering the cargo, and possibly block your view or someone else's.

## Sealed and Containerized Loads

Containerized loads generally are used when freight is carried part way by rail or ship. Delivery by truck occurs at the beginning and/or end of the journey. Some containers have their own tie-down devices or locks that attach directly to a special frame. Others have to be loaded onto

Flatbed trailers: They must be properly secured just like any other cargo. You cannot inspect sealed loads, but you should check that you do not exceed gross weight and axle weight limits

## Transporting Passengers

Passenger vehicle drivers must have a CDL with a passenger endorsement if they drive a vehicle designed to transport more than the state specified

number of persons, including the driver.

A passenger transportation vehicle includes, but is not limited to, a bus, farm labor vehicle, or general public paratransit vehicle when the vehicle is

designed, used, or maintained to carry more than the state specified number of passengers, including the driver, for hire or for profit, or by any nonprofit organization or group.

If you take a driving test in a van designed, used, or maintained to carry 15 persons or less, including the driver, you will be restricted to driving a 15-passenger or less small-size bus.

## Vehicle Inspection

Before driving your bus, you must be sure it is safe. You must review the inspection report made by the previous driver. Only if defects reported earlier have been certified as repaired or repairs not needed, should you sign the previous driver's report. This is your certification that the defects reported earlier have been fixed.

See "Vehicle Inspection Test" section for inspection information and guidelines. Memory aids are shown at the end of section. You may only use one of these when you take your CDL vehicle inspection test for your CDL at DMV. The memory aid cannot include instructions on how to perform the vehicle inspection test.

## Vehicle Systems

Make sure these things are in good working order before driving:

- Service brakes, including air hose couplings (if your bus has a trailer or semitrailer).

- Parking brake.

- Steering mechanism.

- Lights and reflectors.

- Tires (front wheels must not have recapped or regrooved tires).

- Horn.

- Windshield wiper or wipers.

- Rear-vision mirror or mirrors.

- Coupling devices (if present).

- Wheels and rims.

- Emergency equipment.

## Forbidden Hazardous Materials

Buses may carry small-arms ammunition labeled ORM-D, emergency hospital supplies, and drugs. You can carry small amounts of some other hazardous materials if the shipper cannot send them any other way. Buses must never carry:

- Division 2.3 poison gas, liquid Class 6 poison, tear gas, or irritating material.

- More than 100 pounds of solid Class 6 poisons.

- Explosives in the space occupied by people, except small-arms ammunition.

- Labeled radioactive materials in the space occupied by people.

- More than 500 pounds total of allowed hazardous materials, and no more than 100 pounds of any one class.

Riders sometimes board a bus with an unlabeled hazardous material. Do not allow riders to carry on common hazards such as car batteries or gasoline.

Oxygen medically prescribed for, in the possession of a passenger, and in a container designed for personal use is allowed.

Wheelchairs transported on buses (except school buses) must have brakes or other mechanical means of holding still while it is raised or lowered on the wheelchair platform. Batteries must be spill resistant and securely attached to the

Wheelchair: Wheelchairs may not use flammable fuel. School bus wheelchair regulations are in CCR, Title 13 §1293.

## Loading and Unloading

Bus drivers need to consider passenger safety during loading and unloading. Always ensure your passengers are safely on the bus before closing the door(s) and pulling away. Allow passengers enough time to sit down or brace themselves before departing.

## Animals

Transporting animals is prohibited except for certified service, guide, or signal dogs used by physically challenged passengers (California Civil Code (CCC) 54.2).

## Standee Line

No rider may stand forward of the rear of the driver's seat. Buses designed to allow standing

must have a 2-inch line on the floor or some other means of showing riders where they cannot stand. This is called the standee line. All standing riders must stay behind it.

## At Your Destination

When arriving at the destination or intermediate stops, announce:

- The location.

- Reason for stopping.

- Next departure time.

- Bus number.

Remind riders to take carry-ons with them if they get off the bus. If the aisle is on a lower level than the seats, remind riders of the step-down.

## Passenger Supervision

Mention rules about smoking, drinking, or electronic devices at the start of the trip. Explaining the rules at the start will help to avoid trouble later on. While driving, scan the interior of your bus, as well as the road ahead, to the sides, and to the rear. You may have to remind riders about rules, or to keep arms and heads inside the bus.

## At Stops

Riders can stumble when getting on or off and when the bus starts or stops. Caution riders to watch their step when leaving the bus.

Occasionally, you may have a drunk or disruptive rider. You must ensure this rider's safety, as well as that of others. Do not discharge such riders where it would be unsafe for them. It may be safer at the next scheduled stop or a well-lit area where there are other people. Many carriers have guidelines for handling disruptive riders.

## Common Accidents

Most Common Bus Accidents Bus accidents often happen at intersections. Use caution, even if a signal or stop sign controls other traffic. School and mass transit buses sometimes scrape off mirrors or hit passing vehicles when pulling out from a bus stop. Remember the clearance your bus needs, and watch for poles and tree limbs at stops. Know the size of the gap your bus needs to accelerate and merge with traffic. Wait for the gap to open before leaving the stop. Never assume other drivers will brake to give you room when you signal or start to pull out.

## Speed on Curves

Accidents occurring on curves that kill people and destroy buses, result from excessive speed, often when rain or snow has made the road slippery. Every banked curve has a safe "design speed." In good weather, the posted speed is safe for cars but it may be too fast for many buses. With good traction, the bus may roll over. With poor traction, it may slide off the curve. Reduce speed for curves! If your bus leans toward the outside on a banked curve, you are driving too fast.

### Using Your Mirrors

When you use your mirrors while driving on the road, check them quickly. Many buses have convex mirrors that show a wider area than flat mirrors. Remember, these mirrors make things seem smaller and farther away than they really are.

Railroad-Highway Crossing/Stops

### Stop at Railroad Crossings:

- Stop your bus between 15 and 50 feet before crossings.
- Listen and look in both directions for trains. You should open your forward door if it improves your ability to see or hear an approaching train.

- Before crossing after a train has passed, make sure there is not another train coming in the other direction on other tracks.

- If your bus has a manual transmission, never change gears while crossing the tracks.

- You do not have to stop, but must slow down and carefully check for other vehicles:

- At railroad tracks which run alongside and on the roadway within a business or residence district.

- At streetcar crossings where a policeman or flagman is directing traffic.

- If a traffic signal is green.

- At crossings marked as "exempt" or "abandoned."

## About the Test

You are allowed 3 attempts to pass the Knowledge tests and a total of 3 attempts to pass the Skills test. If you fail any segment of the Skills test, it is considered 1 failed attempt. For example, if you failed the vehicle inspection, basic control skills, and road test portions of the Skills test, that is considered 3 failed attempts.

The number of questions on the Knowledge test may differ between states, but you will need to get 80% of the questions correct to pass. You will not be penalized for wrong answers, so even if you don't know the answer to a question, you should guess.

## Road Test

You must take the Skills test using the vehicle type you want to be licensed to drive. During the Skills test, you will be asked to do a pre-trip inspection as well as drive on the road.

To pass the road test portion of the CDL driving performance evaluation

(DPE), you must make no more than 30 errors and no critical driving errors, which will result in an automatic failure. you must drive in a safe and responsible manner and:

- Wear your safety belt.


- Obey all traffic signs, signals, and laws.


- Complete the test without an accident or moving violation.


During the driving test, the examiner will be scoring you on specific driving maneuvers as well as on your general driving behavior. You will follow the directions of the examiner. Directions will be given to you so you will have plenty of time to do what the examiner has asked. You will not be asked to drive in an unsafe manner.

If your test route does not have certain traffic situations, you may be asked to simulate a traffic situation. You will do this by telling the examiner what you are or would be doing if you were in that traffic situation.

Remember: You are allowed a total of 3 attempts to pass the vehicle inspection test, basic control skills test, and road test.

## Note:

A driver must be tested in a truck or bus (as those terms are defined in CFR, Title 49

§390.5), or other single unit vehicle with a GVWR of 26,001 or more, to satisfy the skills testing requirements for a Class B CDL.

## How You Will Be Tested
## Turns

You have been asked to make a turn:


- Check for traffic in all directions.

- Use turn signals and safely get into the lane needed for the turn. As you approach the turn:

- Use turn signals to warn others of your turn.

- Slow down smoothly, change gears as needed to keep power, but do not coast unsafely. Unsafe coasting occurs when your vehicle is out of gear (clutch depressed or gear-shift in Neutral) for more than the length of your vehicle.

## If you must stop before making the turn:

⊿ Come to a smooth stop without skidding.

- Come to a complete stop behind the stop line, crosswalk, or stop sign.

- If stopping behind another vehicle, stop where you can see the rear tires on the vehicle ahead of you (safe gap).

- Do not let your vehicle roll.

- Keep the front wheels aimed straight ahead. When ready to turn:

- Check for traffic in all directions.

- Keep both hands on the steering wheel during the turn.

- Keep checking your mirror to make sure the vehicle does not hit anything on the inside of the turn.

- Vehicle should not move into oncoming traffic.

- Vehicle should finish the turn in the correct lane. After the turn:

- Make sure your turn signal is off.

- Get up to the speed of traffic, use your turn signal, and move into the right- most lane when safe to do so (if not already there).

- Check your mirrors for traffic.

- Intersections

- As you approach an intersection:

- Check for traffic thoroughly in all directions.

- Decelerate gently.

- Brake smoothly and, if necessary, change gears.

- If necessary, come to a complete stop (no coasting) behind any stop signs, signals, sidewalks, or stop lines, and maintain a safe gap behind any vehicle in front of you.

- Your vehicle must not roll forward or backward.

- Note: Do not enter the intersection if there is insufficient space to clear it. When driving through an intersection:

- Check for traffic thoroughly in all directions.

- Decelerate and yield to any pedestrians and traffic in the intersection.

- Do not change lanes while proceeding through the intersection.

Keep your hands on the wheel

## Student Discharge (School Bus)

If you are applying for a school bus endorsement, you will be required to demonstrate loading and unloading students. Please refer to Section: "School Buses" of this manual for procedures on loading and unloading school students.

## General Driving Behaviors

You will be scored on your overall performance in the following general driving behavior categories:

Clutch Usage (for Manual Transmission)

- Always use the clutch to shift.

- Double-clutch when shifting. Do not rev or lug the engine.

- Do not ride the clutch to control speed, coast with the clutch depressed, or "pop" the clutch.

Gear Usage (for Manual Transmission)

- Do not grind or clash the gears.

- Select a gear that does not rev or lug engine.

Do not shift in turns and intersections.

## Brake Usage

- Do not ride or pump the brake.
- Do not brake harshly. Brake smoothly using steady pressure. Lane Usage
- Do not put the vehicle over curbs, sidewalks, or lane markings.

- Stop behind stop lines, crosswalks, or stop signs.

- Complete a turn in the proper lane on a multiple lane road (the vehicle should finish a left turn in the lane directly to the right of the center line).
- Finish a right turn in the right-most (curb) lane.

- Move to or remain in the right-most lane unless lane is blocked.

## Regular Traffic Checks

- Check for traffic regularly.
- Check your mirrors regularly.
- Check your mirrors for traffic before, while in, and after an

intersection.

- Scan and check for traffic in high volume areas and areas where pedestrians are expected to be present.

## ⁜ Use of Turn Signals

- Use your turn signals properly.
- Activate your turn signals when required.
- Activate your turn signals at appropriate times.

Cancel your turn signals upon completion of a turn or lane change.

# Exam Question

1. When should a vehicle be inspected?

a) before, during, and after a trip

b) before and after a trip

c) every 50 miles

d) every 150 miles

2. When should a vehicle be inspected?

a. every 50 miles

b. every 150 miles

c. within the first 50 miles and then every 150 miles

d. within the first 150 miles and then every 3 hours

3. What is the minimum tread depth for tires?

a. 2/32 inch tread for front tires, and 4/32 inch tread for other tires

b. 4/32 inch tread for front tires, and 2/32 inch tread for other tires

c. 1/8 inch tread for front tires, and 1/4 inch tread for other tires

d. 1/4 inch tread for front tires, and 1/8 inch tread for other tires

4. Which of the following is a NOT a steering system part?

a. torque rod

b. drag link

c. tie rod

d. steering arm

5. A vehicle must be equipped with 3 kinds of emergency equipment. Which of the following is NOT one of them?

a. fire extinguisher

b. spare electrical fuses

c. warning devices for parked vehicles

d. first aid kit

6. For use as warning devices for parked vehicles, how many red reflective triangle should you carry?

a. 1

b. 2

c. 3

d. 4

7. Which of the following is NOT a suspension system defect?

a. Spring hangers that allow movement of axle from proper position

b. Missing or broken mounting brackets

c. Missing or broken leaves

d. Leaking shock absorbers

8. During a vehicle inspection test, you should put the starter switch key in your pocket

a. So no one can steal your vehicle

b. So you don't waste gas

c. So the engine doesn't get too hot for you to inspect

9, To test hydraulic brakes for leaks, pump the pedal 3 times. Then apply firm pressure to the pedal and hold for 5 seconds. The pedal should move. If it doesn't, there may be a leak or other problem.

a. True

b. False

10.    Wheel bearing seals should be checked for

a. Rust

b. Correct tread depth

c. Leaks

d. None of the above

11. When backing a vehicle, you should back and turn towards what side?

a. Passenger's side

b. Driver's side

c. Back towards passenger's side and then driver's side

d. Back straight

12.    When stopped on a hill, how do you prevent a vehicle from rolling back?

a. In a manual transmission vehicle, partly engage the clutch before taking foot off the brake.

b. Put on parking brake when necessary. Only release the parking brake when you've applied enough power to keep from rolling back.

c. On a tractor trailer with a brake hand valve, apply the hand valve to keep from rolling back.

d. All of the above

13.    Why is it important to use a helper when backing a vehicle?

a. A helper can stop traffic so you can back out.

b. A helper can you tell you when a vehicle is drifting.

c. There are blind spots you cannot see that a helper can see.

14. What is the most important hand signal you can your helper should agree on?

   a. Go

   b. Stop

   c. Turn left

   d. Turn right

15. What are special conditions in which you should downshift?

   a. Before starting down a hill and before entering a curve

   b. After starting down a hill and after entering a curve

   c. When you engine reaches the top of the tachometer range

   d. All of the above

16. For vehicles with automatic transmissions, you can select a low range to get greater engine braking when going down grades.

   a. True

   b. False

17. You should turn retarders on whenever the road is wet, icy, or snow covered.

   a. True

   b. False

18. What are the ways to know when to shift?

   a. Shift up when going uphill and shift down when going downhill

   b. Shift down when going uphill and shift up when going downhill

c. Shift up or down depending on engine speed (rpm) and road speed (mph)

d. Shift up when entering a curve and shift down when exiting a curve

19. How far ahead should you look?

a) 3 to 5 seconds

b) 5 to 10 seconds

c) 12 to 15 seconds

d) 15 to 20 seconds

20. Where should your reflectors be placed when stopped on a divided highway?

a. Place them 10 feet toward approaching traffic

b. Place them 10 feet, 100 feet, and 200 feet toward approaching traffic

c. Place them 10 feet and 100 feet in front of the vehicle

21. The total stopping distance is reaction distance plus braking distance.

a. True

b. False

22. When doubling your speed, your braking distance is

a. Twice as long

b. Three times as long

c. Four times as long

d. Five times as long

23. Empty trucks require greater stopping distance.

A. True

B. False

24. When water collects on the road and your tires lose contact with the road, this is called

    a. Skidding

    b. Vehicle icing

    c. Spin out

    d. Hydroplaning

25. Hydroplaning is more likely when tire pressure is high.

    a. True

    b. False

26. A thin layer of ice that is clear enough that you can see the road underneath is called

    a. Black ice

    b. Sheet ice

    c. Melting ice

    d. Standing ice

27. To determine how many seconds of following distance space you have, wait until a vehicle ahead passes a shadow on the road, a pavement marking, or some other clear landmark and then count the seconds until you reach the same spot and then double it.

    a. True

    b. False

28. If you are driving a 30 foot vehicle at 55 mph, how many seconds of following distance should you allow?

a. 3 seconds

b. 4 seconds

c. 5 seconds

d. 6 seconds

29. If you are driving a 30 foot vehicle at 35 mph, how many seconds of following distance should you allow?

e. 3 seconds

f. 4 seconds

g. 5 seconds

h. 6 seconds

30. If you are being tailgated, what should you NOT do?

a. Avoid quick changes.

b. Increase your following distance

c. Speed up to put distance between you and the tailgater

d. Avoid tricks such as turning on your tail lights or flashing your brake lights.

31. Drivers signaling a turn may be a hazard.

a. True

b. False

32. The act of operating a motor vehicle in a selfish, bold, or pushy manner, without regard for the rights and safety of others is called:

a. Road rage

b. Distracted driving

c. Aggressive driving

d. None of the above

33. If an aggressive driver is involved in an accident, you should stop immediately and help them; the same as you would for any other driver.

a. True

b. False

34. Most people can tell when they are sleepy or about to fall asleep.

a. True

b. False

35. You must turn your headlights on

a. When visibility is not sufficient to clearly see aperson or vehicle for a distance of 500 feet.

b. An hour after sunset

c. An hour before sunrise

36. If weather conditions require the use of windshield wipers, you must also turn on your headlights.

a. True

b. False

37. Driving-with wet brakes can cause which of the following. Choose all that apply.

a. Engine stalls

b. Wheel lockups

c. Jackknife if you pull a trailer

d. None of the above

38.  When driving in very hot weather, how often should you check the tires?

   a.  Every 3 hours

   b.  Every 150 miles

   c.  Every 2 hours or every 100 miles

   d.  Every 3 hours or every 150 miles

39.  During very hot weather, you should let air out the tires to prevent a blowout.

   a.  True

   b.  False

40.  Antifreeze is only necessary when driving in cold weather conditions.

   a.  True

   b.  False

41.  When is it safe to remove the radiator cap?

   a.  30 minutes after stopping the engine

   b.  When there is no water or steam emanating from the engine

   c.  When you can touch the radiator cap with your bare hand

   d.  The moment you stop the engine

42.  Which of the following factors should you take into consideration when determining a safe speed for going down a long, steep downgrade? Choose all that apply.

   a.  Weather

   b.  Weight of vehicle and cargo

   c.  Length of grade

d. All of the above

43. You should shift your transmission to a low gear before starting a downgrade.

   a. True

   b. False

44. When going down a long and/or steep downgrade, you should release the brakes after your speed has been reduced to:

   a. 5 mph below your "safe" speed

   b. 10 mph below your "safe" speed

   c. Your "safe" speed

   d. Speed limit posted

45. What types of vehicles can get stuck on a railroad crossing? Select all that apply.

   a. Moving van

   b. Car carrier

   c. Possum belly livestock trailer

   d. All of the above

46. How long does it take a typical tractor trailer unit to clear a double track?

   a. More than 12 seconds

   b. More than 13 seconds

   c. More than 14 seconds

   d. More than 15 seconds

47. If there is no white stop line painted on the pavement of a railroad crossing, vehicles that are required to stop must stop:

a. No closer than 10 feet or more than 50 feet from the nearest rail

b. No closer than 10 feet or more than 30 feet from the nearest rail

c. No closer than 15 feet or more than 50 feet from the nearest rail

d. No closer than 15 feet or more than 30 feet from the nearest rail

48. Stopping is not always the safest thing to do in an emergency.

a. True

b. False

49. If an oncoming driver had drifted into your lane, what should you do?

a. Immediately press on the brakes

b. Move to your right

c. Move to your left

d. None of the above

50. If your brakes fail on a long downgrade, your best bet is to

a. Find an escape ramp

b. Exit the vehicle

c. Pump the brakes

d. Shift into a lower gear

51. What should you do if a tire blows out?

a. Put the brakes on hard to stop quickly

b. Downshift into a lower gear

c. Hold steering wheel firmly and stay off the brake

d. B and C

52. What is the purpose of an anti-lock braking system?

    a. To increase your normal braking capability

    b. To keep your wheels from locking up during hard brake applications

    c. To shorten you're stopping distance

    d. All of the above

53. The Anti-lock Braking System is only activated when wheels are about to lock up.

    a. True

    b. False

54. In the case of towed units manufactured before ABS was required by the DOT, how do you tell if the vehicle is equipped with ABS?

    a. Look under the vehicle for the ECU and wheel speed sensor wires coming from the back of the brakes.

    b. Look for a yellow ABS malfunction lamp on the instrument panel

    c. Look for a yellow ABS malfunction lamp on the front or rear corner

    d. There is no way to tell other than to call the manufacturer

55. There are special braking procedures to follow when braking in a vehicle equipped with an ABS system.

    a. True

    b. False

56. How do you correct a drive wheel braking skid?

    a. Stop braking and stop turning

    b. Stop braking and counter steer

    c. Press the brakes and keep steering wheel straight

    d. Press the brakes and counter steer

57. If you are stopping to help in an accident, you should park near the accident.

   a. True

   b. False

58. All of the following can be causes of vehicle fires, except:

   a. Improper use of flares

   b. Under inflated tires

   c. Improperly sealed cargo

   d. None of the above

59. A regular dry chemical fire extinguisher can be used on what class of fire?

   a. A

   b. B

   c. C

   d. B and C

60. Water can be used on which of the following fire types?

   a. Wood, paper, or cloth

   b. Electrical

   c. Gasoline

   d. Electrical and gasoline

61. When aiming the fire extinguisher, you should:

   a. Aim to the right of the fire

   b. Aim to the left of the fire

c. Aim at the source or base of the fire

d. Aim at the flames

62. The law prohibits driving under the influence of controlled substances, which includes a variety of prescriptions and over-the- counter drugs such as cold medicines that may make a driver drowsy or affect driving ability.

a. True

b. False

63. You may NEVER drink while on duty, nor consume any intoxicating beverage, regardless of its alcohol content, within how many hours before going on duty?

a. 1

b. 2

c. 3

d. 4

64. What are placards used for?

a. To warn others of hazardous materials

b. To warn others that a vehicle will be travelling below the speed limit

c. To warn others of a wide load

d. To warn others that a vehicle will be making sudden stops

65. All placarded vehicles must have at least how many identical placards displayed?

a. 1

b. 2

c. 3

d. 4

66. Not all vehicles carrying hazardous materials need to have placards.

a. True

b. False

67. You can drive a vehicle that carries hazardous materials if it does not required placards, even if you do not have a Haz-Mat Endorsement

a. True

b. False

68. How often must you check cargo?

a. Within the first 100 miles after beginning a trip

b. After you have driven for 2 hours or 100 miles

c. A and B

d. None of the above

69. The value specified by the manufacturer as the loaded weight of a single vehicle is

a. Gross vehicle weight

b. Gross combination weight

c. Gross vehicle weight rating

d. Gross combination weight rating

70. Under what conditions may it not be safe to operate a vehicle at legal maximum weights?

a. Bridges

b. Mountains

c. Bad weather

d. B and C

71. What can happen if your front axles are under loaded?

a. It can cause hard steering

b. It can make the steering axle weight too light to steer safely

c. It can cause poor traction

d. It can increase your risk of a rollover

72. What is the minimum number of tie-downs for any flatbed load?

a. 2

b. 4

c. 6

d. 8

73. What is the minimum number of tie-downs for a 40 foot load?

2

e. 3

f. 4

g. 5

74. Why must cargo be covered on an open bed?

a. To prevent theft

b. To protect people from spilled cargo

c. To protect cargo from the weather

d. B and C

75. You cannot inspect sealed loads, but you should check that you do not exceed gross weight and axle weight limits.

    a. True

    b. False

76. Which of the following cargo need special attention?

    a. Dry bulk

    b. Hanging meat

    c. Livestock

    d. All of the above

77. To avoid glare from oncoming vehicles, you should

    a. Look to the left

    b. Look to the right

    c. Look up

    d. Look down

78. When driving at night, use high beams when

    a. Never use your high beams

    b. You are not within 200 feet of an approaching vehicle

    c. You are not within 500 feet of an approaching vehicle

    d. You are not within 1000 feet of an approaching vehicle

79. When driving in fog in the daytime, you should use your high beams.

    a. True

    b. False

80. When temperature drops, bridges will freeze before the roads will.

a. True

b. False

81. When large vehicles are being driven in a caravan on the open highway, at least how many feet must be left between them to allow other vehicles to overtake and pass them?

a. 50 feet

b. 100 feet

c. 150 feet

d. 200 feet

82. How can you quickly sober up?

a. Drink coffee (or something else with lots of caffeine) to counteract effects of alcohol

b. Drink more water so that more alcohol will be eliminated through urine

c. Eat more food to absorb the alcohol in your stomach

d. None of the above

83. All of the following are signs of a tire failure, except:

a. A loud "bang"

b. Vibrations

c. Steering that feels light

d. Vehicle starts to slide back and forth

84. You should apply your brakes when turning.

a. True

b. False

85. When stopping at a railroad highway crossing, you should turn on your 4 way emergency flashers.

   a. True

   b. False

86. What type of railroad crossing has a traffic control device installed to regulate traffic at the crossing?

   a. Passive crossing

   b. Controlled crossing

   c. Active crossing

   d. Guarded crossing

87. Why should you check v-belt tightness in your vehicle?

   a. Loose belts will not turn the water pump and/or fan properly. This will result in overheating.

   b. Loose belts will cause the engine to "knock".

   c. Loose belts will cause the engine to stall.

   d. All of the above

88. Bright lights at night can cause dirt on your windshield or mirrors to create a glare of its own, blocking your view.

   a. True

   b. False

89. If your driver license says corrective lenses are required, it is illegal to move a vehicle without corrective lenses.

   a. True

   b. Flese

90. What is normal engine oil pressure when idling?

a. 5 to 20 psi

b. 20 to 35 psi

c. 35 to 75 psi

d. 75 to 100 psi

91. What is normal engine oil pressure when operating a vehicle?

a. 5 to 20 psi

b. 20 to 35 psi

c. 35 to 75 psi

d. 75 to 100 psi

92. Air pressure in a vehicle should build from 50 to 90 psi within?

a. Seconds

b. 3 minutes

c. 5 minutes

d. 10 minutes

93. All of the following defects can let poison fumes into the cab or sleeper berth, except

a. Broken leaf spring

b. Broken exhaust pipe

c. Broken mounting brackets

d. All of the above

94. If you operate a CDL required vehicle in interstate commerce, the vehicle, with few exceptions, is required to be registered under the

a. IRS

b. IRP

c. IFTA

d. B and C

95. Which of the following is considered a serious traffic violation?

a. Excessive speeding

b. Following a vehicle too closely

c. Improper or erratic lane changes

d. All of the above

96. If the Anti-Lock Braking System is working properly, the ABS light will stay on.

a. True

b. False

97. Clearing under a bridge when your CMV was loaded does not mean it will clear it when you are empty.

a. True

b. False

98. For a cargo fire in a van or box trailer, you should open the doors to cool the fire.

a. True

b. False

99. When transporting hazardous materials, shipping papers must be kept in or on:

a. A pouch on the driver's door

b. Clear view within reach while driving

c.  The driver's seat when out of the vehicle

d.  All of the above

100.  What is used in the front, back, and/or sides of a piece of cargo to keep it from sliding?

a.  Blocking

b.  Bracing

c.  Chocking

# Answers

1. A. A vehicle inspection should be done before, during, and after a trip. After the trip, day, or tour of duty, you should fill out a report listing any problems you found. During a tri you should inspect the vehicle within the first 50 miles and then every 150 miles or 3 hours (whichever comes first).

2. C. A vehicle inspection should be done before, during, and after a trip. After the trip, day, or tour of duty, you should fill out a report listing any Problems you found. During a trip, you should inspect the vehicle within the first 50 miles and then every 150 miles or 3 hours (whichever comes first).

3. B. There should be at least 4/32 inch tread depth in every major groove on the front tires; 2/32 inch tread on other tires. No fabric should show through the tread or sidewall.

4. A. A torque rod is part of the suspension system, not the steering system.

5. D. Vehicles must be equipped with the following emergency equipment: Fire extinguisher(s); Spare electrical fuses (unless equipped with                circuit breakers); Warning devices for parked vehicles (for example, 3 red reflective warning triangles, 6 fuses, or 3 liquid burning flares).

6. C. Warning devices for parked vehicles (3 red reflective warning triangles, 6 fuses, or 3 liquid burning flares)

7. B. Missing or broken mounting brackets are exhausting system defects.

8. D. During a vehicle inspection test, you should put the starter switch key in your pocket so someone else will not move the truck while you are under it.

9. B. To test hydraulic brakes for leaks, pump the pedal 3 times. Then apply firm pressure to the pedal and hold for 5 seconds. The pedal

should not move. If it does, there may be a leak or other problem.

10. C. Wheel bearing seals should be checked for leaks.

11. B. When backing a vehicle, back towards the driver's side so you can see better.

12. D. All of the above are ways to prevent a vehicle from rolling back when stopped on a hill.

13. C. You should use a helper because there are blind spots that you cannot see. The helper should stand near the back of your vehicle where you can see the helper.

14. B. Before you begin backing a vehicle, you and your helper should agree on a set of hand signals; the most important signal being the signal for "stop".

15. A. You should downshift before starting down a hill and before entering a curve. You should upshift when the engine reaches the top of the tachometer range.

16. A. For vehicles with automatic transmissions, you can select a low range to get greater engine braking when going down grades. The lower ranges prevent the transmission from shifting up beyond the selected gear. It is very important to use this braking effect when doing down grades.

17. B. When your drive wheels have poor traction, the retarder may cause them to skid. You should turn off the retarder whenever the road is wet, icy, or snow covered.

18. C. Pay attention to the engine speed (rpm) and road speed (mph) to know when to shift.

19. C. You should look ahead 12 to 15 seconds; this does not mean you shouldn't pay attention to things that are near. You need to shift your attention back and forth, near and far.

20. B. If you must stop on or by a one way or divided highway, place warning devices 10 feet, 100 feet, and 200 feet toward approaching

traffic. If you stop on a 2 lane road carrying traffic in both directions or on an undivided highway, place warning devices within 10 feet of the front or rear corners and 100 feet behind and ahead of the vehicle.

21. B. The total stopping distance is perception distance plus reaction distance plus braking distance. Perception distance is the distance a vehicle travels from the time your eyes sees a hazard until your brain recognizes it. Reaction distance is the distance a vehicle travels before you physically hit the brakes in response to a hazard seen. Braking distance is the distance a vehicle travels while you are braking.

22. C. When doubling your speed, your braking distance is 4 times as long. If you triple your speed, the braking distance is 9 times as long.

23. A. The heavier the vehicle, the more work the brakes must do to stop it and the more heat they absorb. The brakes, tires, springs, and shock absorbers on heavy vehicles are designed to work best when the vehicle is fully loaded. Empty trucks require greater stopping distances because an empty vehicle has less traction.

24. D. When water or slush collects on the road when this happens, your vehicle can hydroplane. It is like water skiing-the tires lose their contact with the road and have little or no traction. You may not be able to steer or brake. You can regain control by releasing the accelerator and pushing in the clutch. This will slow your vehicle and let the wheels turn freely. If the vehicle is hydroplaning, do not use the brakes to slow down. If the drive wheels start to skid, push in the clutch to let them turn freely.

25. B. Hydroplaning is more likely when tire pressure is low or tread is worn.

26. A. Black ice is a thin layer of ice that is clear enough that you can see the road underneath. Any time the temperature is below freezing and the road looks wet, look out for black ice.

27. B. To determine how many seconds of following distance space you have, wait until a vehicle ahead passes a shadow on the road, a pavement marking, or some other clear landmark and then count the seconds until you reach the same spot. There is no need to double the number of seconds.

28. B. You need at least 1 second for each 10 feet of vehicle length at speeds below 40 mph. At speeds greater than 40 mph, add an extra second.

29. A. You need at least 1 second for each 10 feet of vehicle length at speeds below 40 mph. At speeds greater than 40 mph, add an extra second.

30. C. Do not speed up. It is safer to be tailgated at a low speed than a high speed.

31. A. Drivers signaling a turn may be a hazard because they may slow more than expected or stop suddenly.

32. C. The act of operating a motor vehicle in a selfish, bold, or pushy manner, without regard for the rights and safety of others is called aggressive driving. The act of operating a motor vehicle with the intent of doing harm to others or physically assaulting a driver or their vehicle is called road rage.

33. B. If an aggressive driver is involved in an accident, you should a safe distance from the accident scene and wait for the police to arrive.

34. B. Many people cannot tell when they are about to fall asleep. If you notice any signs of fatigue, do not try to "power through"; stop driving and go to sleep for the night or take a 15 - 20 minute nap.

35. D. You must turn your headlights on a half hour after sunset and a half hour before sunrise; when visibility is not sufficient to clearly see a person or vehicle for a distance for 1000 feet; and if snow, rain, fog, or other hazardous weather condition requires the use of windshield wipers.

36. A. You must turn your headlights on a half hour after sunset and a half hour before sunrise; when visibility is not sufficient to clearly see a person or vehicle for a distance for 1000 feet; and if snow, rain, fog, or other hazardous weather condition require the use of windshield

wipers.

37. B, C. Driving with wet brakes can cause lack of braking power, wheel lockups, pulling to one side and jackknife if you pull a trailer.

38. C. When driving in very hot weather, you should inspect the tires every 2 hours or every 150 miles. Air pressure increases with temperature. If a tire is too hot to touch, remain stopped until the tire cools off. Otherwise the tire may blow out or catch fire.

39. B. During very hot weather, do not let air out of tires or the tire pressure will be too low when the tires cool off.

40. B. Antifreeze helps the engine under hot as well as cool conditions.

41. C. Never remove the radiator cap or any part of a pressurized system until the system has cooled. If you can touch the part with your bare hands, it is probably cool enough to open.

42. D. When going down long, steep downgrade, consider the following factors: total weight of vehicle and cargo, length of grade, steepness of grade, road conditions, and weather.

43. A. You should shift your transmission to a low gear before starting a downgrade. Do not try to downshift after your speed has already built up. You will not be able to shift into a lower gear.

44. A. The proper braking technique when going down a long and/or steep downgrade is to 1. Apply the brakes just hard enough to feel a definite slowdown 2. Release brakes after speed has been reduced to 5 mph below your "safe" speed 3. When your speed has increased to your "safe" speed, repeat steps 1 and 2.

45. D. The following vehicles can get stuck on a raised crossing: Low slung units (lowboy, car carrier, moving van, possum belly livestock trailer); single axle tractor pulling a long trailer with its landing gear set to accommodate a tandem axle tractor

46. D. It takes a typical tractor trailer at least 14 seconds to clear 1 track and

more than 15 seconds to clear a double track.

47. C. If there is no white stop line painted on the pavement of a railroad crossing, vehicles that are required to stop must stop no closer than 15 feet or more than 50 feet from the nearest rail.

48. A. Stopping is not always the safest thing to do in an emergency. When you do not have enough room to stop, you should steer away from the hazard ahead.

49. B. If an oncoming driver has drifted into your lane, a move to your right is your best bet. If that driver realizes what has happened, the natural response is for them to return to their own lane. Also, no one is likely to be driving on the shoulder, but someone may be passing on the left.

50. A. If your brakes fail on a long downgrade, your best bet is an escape ramp. Ramps are usually located a few miles from the top of the downgrade. If no escape ramp is available, take the least hazardous escape route you can, such as an open field or a side road that flattens out or turns uphill.

51. C. If a front tire fails, it can twist the steering wheel out of your hands. To prevent this, you need to keep a firm grip on the steering wheel with both hands at all times. Braking when a tire has failed could cause loss of control. Unless you are about to run into something, stay off the brake until the vehicle has slowed down then brake gently, pull off the road, and stop.

52. B. An anti-lock braking system is a computerized system that keeps your wheels from locking up during hard brake applications. It does not increase

or decrease your normal braking capability. ABS does not shorten your stopping distance, but helps keeps the vehicle under control during hard

braking.

53. A

54. A

55. B. When you drive a vehicle equipped with ABS, brake as you normally do. The only exception is if you drive a straight truck or combination with working ABS on all axles, you can fully apply the brakes in an emergency stop. If your ABS system is not working, you should still have normal braking functionality.

56. B. To correct a drive wheel braking skid, you should stop   braking and counter steer. Taking your foot off the brakes, will allow the rear wheels to roll again and keep the rear wheels from skidding. As a vehicle turns back on course, it has a tendency to keep on turning. Unless you counter steer, you may begin skidding in the opposite direction.

57. B. If you are stopping to help in an accident, you should park away from the accident. The area immediately around the accident will be needed for emergency vehicles.

58. D. Spilled fuel, improper use of flares, under-inflated tires, dual tires that touch, short circuits, loose connections, driver smoking, improper fueling, loose fuel connections, flammable cargo, improperly sealed or loaded cargo, and poor ventilation can all be causes of vehicle fires.

59. D. A regular dry chemical fire extinguisher can be used  on class B (Gasoline, Oil, Grease, and Other Greasy Liquids) or class C (Electrical Equipment) fires.

60. A. Water can be used on wood, paper, or cloth fires. Never use water on electrical fires (can cause shock) or gasoline fires (it will spread the flames).

61. C. When using a fire extinguisher, stay as far away as possible and aim at the source or base of the fire.

62. A. Any medication, prescribed or not, that affects your driving

ability is prohibited. Use of a drug prescribed by a doctor is permitted if the doctor informs the driver that it would not affect the driver's safe driving abilities.

63. D

64. A. A placard is used to warn others of hazardous material. The placard will display a 4 digit code (identification numbers) that first responders can use to identify hazardous materials.

65. D. All placarded vehicles must have at least 4 identical placards displayed: one each on the front, rear, left, and right side. They must be readable from all 4 directions. They must be at least 10 &frac34; inches square, turned upright on a point, in a diamond shape.

66. A

67. A

68. D. You must inspect your cargo within the first 50 miles after beginning a trip; after you have driven for 3 hours or 150 miles; and after every break you take during your trip.

69. C. Gross vehicle weight rating is the value specified by the manufacturer as the loaded weight of a single vehicle. Gross vehicle weight is the total weight of a single vehicle including its load. Gross combination weight is the total weight of a combination of vehicles including the load. Gross combination weight rating is the value specified by the manufacturer as the loaded weight of a combination vehicle.

70. D. During bad weather or in mountains, it may not be safe to operate at legal maximum weights.

71. B. Too much weight on the steering axle can cause hard steering. Under-loaded front axles can make the steering axle weight too light to steer safely. Too little weight on the driving axles can cause poor traction. The drive wheels may spin easily. Weight that is loaded so there is a high center of gravity increases chances of a rollover.

72. A. No matter how small the cargo, it should have at least 2 tie downs. Cargo should have at least 1 tie-down for each 10 feet of cargo.

73. C. Cargo should have at least 1 tie down for each 10 feet of cargo, with an absolute minimum of 2 tie-downs.

74. D. Cargo on an open bed should be covered to protect people from spilled cargo and to protect cargo from the weather.

75. A

76. D. Dry bulk, hanging meat, livestock, oversized loads, projecting loads, special markings needed, piggyback trailers all require special attention.

77. B. Do not look directly at lights of oncoming traffic, look slightly to the right.

78. C

79. B. When driving in fog in the daytime, you should use your low beam headlights and fog lights.

80. A

81. B

82. D. Nothing but time will sober you up.

83. C. A loud "bang", vibrations, steering that feels heavy, and a vehicle that starts to slide back and forth (or "fishtail") are signs of a tire failure.

84. B. Do not apply the brakes while you are turning. It is very easy to lock your wheels while turning. If that happens, you may skid out of control.

85. A

86. C. An active crossing is a type of railroad crossing that has a traffic Control device installed to regulate traffic. A passive crossing has no traffic control device.

87. A

88. A

89. A

90. A. Engine oil pressure should come up to normal within a few

seconds after the engine is started. When idling, normal oil pressure is 5 to 20 psi when operating, normal engine oil pressure is 35 to 75 psi

91. C. Engine oil pressure should come up to normal within a few seconds after the engine is started. When idling, normal oil pressure is 5 to 20 psi when operating, normal engine oil pressure is 35 to 75 psi

92. B

93. A. A broken leaf spring is a suspension system defect. Exhaust system defects can let poison fumes into the cab or sleeper berth.

94. D. If you operate a CDL required vehicle in interstate commerce, the vehicle, with few exceptions, is required to be registered under the International Registration Plan (IRP) and under the International Fuel Tax Agreement (IFTA). These federally mandated programs provide for the equitable collection and distribution of vehicle license fees and motor fuel taxes for vehicles traveling throughout the 48 contiguous U.S. states and 10 Canadian provinces.

95. D. Excessive speeding (15 mph over speed limit), reckless driving, improper or erratic lane changes, following a vehicle too closely, traffic offenses committed in a CMV in connection with a fatal traffic accident, driving a CMV without obtaining a CDL or having a CDL in the driver's possession, and driving a CMV without the proper class of CDL and/or endorsements are all considered serious traffic violations.

96. B. If the Anti-Lock Braking System is working properly, the ABS light should come on and then turn off.

97. A. The weight of a cargo van changes its height. An empty van is higher than a loaded one.

98. B. For a cargo fire in a van or box trailer, you should keep the doors shut. Opening the doors will supply with fire with oxygen and can cause it to burn very fast.

99. A

100. A. Blocking is used in the front, back, and/or sides of a piece of

cargo to keep it from sliding. Bracing is also used to prevent movement of cargo; it goes from the upper part of the cargo to the floor and/or walls of the cargo compartment.

101.

# Passenger Transport Practice Test

1. Which of the following items in the interior of a bus should you always check before driving?

   a. Check that aisles and stairwells are clear

   b. Check that emergency exit handles are working

   c. Each handhold and railing are in working condition

   d. All of the above

2. Which of the following hazardous material can you transport by bus?

   a. Small arms ammunition labeled ORM-D

   b. Explosives

   c. Gasoline

   d. None of the above

3. Which of the following can never be transported by bus?

   a. Liquid pesticides

   b. 25 pounds of solid class 6 poisons

   c. Small arms ammunition labeled ORM-D

   d. All of the above

4. All standing riders must stand

   a. Behind the first row of seats

   b. Behind the standee line

   c. Behind the driver

   d. None of the above

5.  How far from a railroad crossing should you stop?

    a.  5 to 10 feet

    b.  10 to 15 feet

    c.  15 to 50 feet

    d.  50 to 100 feet

6.  Disruptive passengers must be dealt with and dropped off immediately.

    a.  True

    b.  False

7.  You must stop at all drawbridges.

    a.  True

    b.  False

8.  How far away do you need to stop from a drawbridge?

    a.  10 feet

    b.  25 feet

    c.  50 feet

    d.  100 feet

9.  Which of the following are prohibited practices?

    a.  Fueling your bus with riders on board, unless absolutely necessary

    b.  Talking and engaging with riders

    c.  Towing or pushing a disabled bus with riders on board, unless absolutely necessary

    d.  All of the above

10. The rear door of a transit bus has to be open to put on the parking brake.

    a.

    b. False

11. A bus must be equipped with a fire extinguisher, emergency reflectors, and spare electrical fuses, unless equipped with circuit breakers.

    a. True

    b. False

12. Riders are allowed to leave carry-on baggage in the aisle way.

    a. True

    **b.** False

# Passenger Transport Practice Test Answers

1. D. Always check the interior of the bus before driving. Check that aisles and stairwells are clear; each handhold and railing is in working condition; floor covering; signaling devices are working; emergency exit handles are working.

2. A. Buses may carry small arms ammunition labeled ORM-D, emergency hospital supplies, and drugs.

3. A. Buses must never carry Division 2.3 poison gas, liquid Class 6 poison, tear gas, more than 100 pounds of solid Class 6 poisons, explosives, radioactive materials, more than 500 pounds total of allowed hazardous materials, and no more than 100 pounds of any one class. Pesticides are a class 6 poison.

4. B. The standee line is a 2 inch line on the floor that all standing riders must be behind.

5. C

6. B. All passengers, disruptive or not, must be dropped off at a safe location.

7. B. You only need to stop at drawbridges that do not have a signal light or traffic control attendant. You don't need to stop, but must slow down if there is a traffic light showing green or there is a bridge attendant.

8. C

9. D

10. B. Transit buses may have a brake and accelerator interlock system. The interlock applies the brakes and holds the throttle in idle when the rear door is open. The interlock releases when you close the rear door. Do not use this safety feature in place of the parking brake.

11. A

12. B. There should be nothing in the aisle that may trip riders or prevent riders from exiting.

# Air Brakes Practice Test

1. Compressed air usually has some water and some compressor oil in it, Which is bad for the air brake system The water can freeze in cold weather and cause brake failure.

   a. True

   b. False

2. What gauge tells you how much pressure is in the air tanks?

   a. Application pressure gauge

   b. Low air pressure warning

   c. Supply pressure gauge

   d. None of the above

3. Which vehicles must have low air pressure warning signals?

   a. Vehicles built after 1998

   b. Vehicles built after 2005

   c. Warning signals are optional

   d. All vehicles with air brakes must have low air pressure warning signals

4. This type of brake is a parking brake held on by mechanical force.

   a. Wedge brake

   b. Spring brake

   c. Disc brake

   d. None of the above

5. Front wheel braking is good under all conditions.

   a. True

   b. False

6. What brake system has 2 separate air brake systems, which use a single set of brake controls?

   a. Dual air brake system

   b. Twin air brake system

   c. Double air brake system

   d. Anti-lock brake system

7. What part of the braking system is used to adjust the brakes?

   a. Brake adjuster

   b. Slack adjuster

   c. Drum adjuster

   d. Disc adjuster

8. A slack adjuster needs adjustment if it moves more than how many inches from where the push rod attaches to it?

   a. 1

   b. 2

   c. 3

   d. 4

9. To test the low pressure warning signal, all of the following must be done except:

   a. Engine may be on or off

   b. Engine must be on

c. Key must be in "on" or "battery charge" position

d. Fan off the air pressure by rapidly applying and releasing the foot brake

10. To test that spring brakes come on automatically, all of the following are true accept:

a. Chock the wheels

   a. Release the parking brake valve

   b. Reduce the air pressure by stepping on and off the brake pedal

   c. Parking brake valve should pop out when air pressure falls to 55 to 75 psi

11. What is the maximum leakage rate for single vehicles in the Applied Leakage Test?

   a. 1 psi

   b. 3 psi

   c. 4 psi

   d. 6 psi

12. What is the maximum leakage for a combination of 2 vehicles in the Applied Leakage Test?

   a. 1 psi

   b. 3 psi

   c. 4 psi

   d. 6 psi

13. What is the maximum leakage for a combination of 3 or more vehicles in the Applied Leakage Test?

   a. 1 psi

b. 3 psi

c. 4 psi

d. 6 psi

14. You should be in the proper gear before starting down a hill.

a. True

b. False

15. Which of the following factors can cause brakes to fade or fail?

a. Using brakes too much without relying on the engine braking effect

b. Excessive heat

c. Brakes that are out of adjustment

d. All of the above.

16. The use of brakes on a long, steep downgrade is only a supplement to the braking effect of the engine.

a. True

b. False

17. How often should you drain your air tanks?

a. After every trip

b. Before every trip

c. At the end of each day of driving

d. At the beginning of each day of driving

18. There are special braking procedures you must follow when driving a tractor trailer combination with ABS?

a. True

b. False

19. What pumps air into the air storage tanks?

 a. Air compressor

 b. Air compressor governor

 c. CamLaster

 d. None of the above

20. If the safety valve releases air, the air braking system is working properly.

 a. True

b. False

21. Never push the brake pedal down when the spring brakes are on.

 a. True

 b. False

22. What keeps air from going out if the air compressor develops a leak?

 a. Safety valve

 b. One way check valve

 c. Highway valve

 d. Emergency valve

23. For dual air systems, air pressure should build

 a. From 50 to 90 psi within 45 seconds

 b. From 50 to 90 psi within 3 minutes

 c. From 85 to 100 psi within 45 seconds

d.From 85 to 100 psi within 3 minutes

24. The air compressor should cut out no higher than_ psi and should cut in no lower than___ psi for a bus, and no lower than psi for trucks.

   a. 140, 85, 100

   b. 140, 75, 100

   c. 120, 85, 100

   d. 120, 75, 100

25. Do not use parking brakes if the brakes are very hot or if the brakes are very wet in freezing temperatures.

   a. True

   b. False

26. Front wheel brakes are only good for driving under wet or icy conditions.

   a. True

   b. False

27. While driving down long, steep downgrades, your brakes

   a. Are the main braking mechanism

   b. Act as a supplement to the breaking effect of your engine

   c. None of the above

# Air Brakes Practice Test Answers

1. A

2. C The supply pressure gauge tells you how much pressure is in the air tanks. The application pressure gauge shows you how much air pressure you are applying to the brakes.

3. D. All vehicles with air brakes must have low air pressure warning signals.

4. B. A spring break is a parking brake held on by mechanical force. In a Wedge brake, the brake chamber push rod pushed a wedge directly between the ends of 2 brake shoes. In a disc brake, air pressure acts on a brake chamber and a slack adjuster.

5. A. Test have shown that front wheel skids from braking are unlikely, even on ice.

6. A

7. B. The slack adjuster is the part of the braking system used to adjust the brakes.

8. A. To check slack adjusters, park on level ground and chock the wheels to prevent it from moving. Release the parking brakes so you can move the slack adjusters. Pull on each slack adjuster; if they move more than 1 inch, they need to be adjusted.

9. B. To test the low pressure warning signal, the engine may be "on" or "off", but the key must in the "on" or "battery charge" position. Fan off the air pressure by rapidly applying and releasing the foot brake The warning will activate when it falls between 55 to 75 psi; but may activate at higher pressure (80-85 psi).

10. D. Parking brake valve should pop out when air pressure falls to 20 to 45 psi.

11. B

12. C. The maximum leakage for a combination of 2 vehicles is 4 psi per

minute. If the towed vehicles are not equipped with air brakes, the maximum leakage is 3 psi.

13. D

14. A. You should be in the proper gear before starting down a hill; you will not be able to shift to a lower gear once the vehicle picks up speed.

15. D

16. A

17. C

18. B. You should brake as you normally would without ABS.

19. A. The air compressor pumps air into the air storage tanks. The air compressor governor controls when the air compressor will pump air into the tanks.

20. B. The safety valve protects the tank and the rest of the system from too much pressure. It is installed in the first tank the air compressor pumps air into. The valve is set to open at 150 psi. If the safety valve releases air, something is wrong and it should be fixed by a mechanic.

21. A. Never push the brake pedal down when the spring brakes are on. If you do, the brakes could be damaged by the combined forces of the springs

22. B. The one way check valve allows air to flow in one direction only and keeps air from going out if the air compressor develops a leak. All air tanks on air broken vehicles must have a check valve located between the air compressor ad the first reservoir.

23. C. For dual air systems, air pressure should build from 85 to 95 psi within 45 seconds. For single air systems, air pressure should build from 50 to 90 psi   within 3 minutes.

24. A

25. A. If parking brakes are used when brakes are very hot, they can be damaged. If parking brakes are used in freezing temperatures when the brakes are very wet, they can freeze so the vehicle cannot move

26. B. Front wheel brakes are good for driving in all weather  conditions.

27.  B. Your brakes act as a supplement to the braking effect of your engine and cannot completely compensate for driving down steep grades in too high of a gear.

# Combination Vehicles Practice Test

1. What are things you can do to reduce rollover risks?

   a. Keep cargo as close to the center of the vehicle as possible

   b. Keep cargo as close to the ground as possible

   c. Drive slowly around turns

   d. All of the above

2. When you turn suddenly while pulling doubles, which trailer is most likely to turn over?

   a. Front trailer

   b. Rear trailer

   c. They are equally likely to turn over

3. You should use the trailer handbrake to straighten out a jackknifing trailer.

   a. True

   b. False

4. When a vehicle goes around a corner and the rear wheels follow a different path than the front wheels, this is called

   a. Jackknifing

   b. Crack-the-whip

   c. Off-tracking

   d. None of the above

5.   When backing a trailer, you should

a. Turn the wheel in the direction you want to go

b. Turn the wheel in the opposite direction of where you want to go

6.   Always keep the wheel straight
The earliest and best way to recognize that the trailer has started to skid is by

a. Seeing it in your mirrors

b. Feeling whether your vehicle wobbles

c. Hearing the trailer move

d. Steering becomes harder

7.   The trailer hand valve should be used only to test the trailer brakes.

a. True

b. False

8.   What is the purpose of the trailer air supply control?

a. Control "emergency" valves

b. Controls the emergency brakes on combination vehicles

c. Keeps air in the tractor or truck brake system should the trailer break away or develop a bad leak

d. None of the above

9.   The service line supplies air to the trailer air tanks.

a. True

b. False

10.   What supplies air to the trailer air tanks and controls the emergency brakes on combination vehicles?

a. Service line

b. Emergency air line

c. Air supply control

d. Tractor protection valve

11.  In vehicles without spring brakes, it is very important for safety that you use wheel chocks when you park trailers.

a. True

   12. False

12. What part permits closing the airlines off when another trailer is not being towed?

a. Shut off valve

b. Tractor protection valve

c. Hose couplers

d. Air supply control

e.

13.  When coupling, if the trailer is too low, the tractor may strike and damage the trailer nose.

a. True

b. False

14.  After coupling, how much space should be between the upper and lower fifth wheel?

a. 1 inch

b. 2 inches

c. 5 inches

d. No space

15. When inspecting the coupling, you should look into the back of the fifth wheel to see if it locked onto the kingpin.

   a. True

   b. False

16. To drive, you should raise the landing gear

   a. Only until it just lifts off the pavement

   b. Until it is 5 inches off the ground

   c. All the way up.

17. Which shut-off valves should be closed?

   a. Shut off valves at the back of the last trailer

   b. Shut off valves on the trailers

   c. Shut off valves on the dollies

   d. All of the above

18. To check that air flows to all the trailers, you open the emergency line shut-off valve at the rear of the last trailer; you should hear air escaping. Open the service line valve to check that service pressure goes through all the trailers.

   a. True

   b. False

19. When testing the tractor protection valve,

   a. You should hear air escaping

   b. The air supply control should pop out when air pressure falls into a manufacturer specified range

   c. The air supply control should pop out when air pressure rises into a manufacturer specified range

d. None of the above

20. To test the trailer emergency brakes, you should pull out the trailer air service line.

a. True

b. False

# Combination Vehicles Practice Test Answers

1. D. When more cargo is piles higher up, the "center of gravity" moves up which increases the chances of rollover? To reduce risk of rollovers, keep cargo centered and as close to the ground as possible. Rollovers can happen when you turn too fast.

2. b. "Rearward amplification" causes the crack-the-whip effect. The rear trailer is twice as likely to turn over as the tractor.

3. b. Do not use the trailer handbrake to straighten out a jackknifing trailer. This is the wrong thing to do since the brakes on the trailer wheels caused the skid in the first place. Release the brakes to get traction back

4. c. When a vehicle goes around a corner and the rear wheels follow a different path than the front wheels, this is called off-tracking

5. b. When backing a car, straight truck, or bus, turn the  wheel in the direction you want to go. When backing a trailer, turn the wheel in the opposite direction. Once the trailer starts to turn, turn the wheel the other way to follow the trailer.

6. A. The earliest and best way to recognize that the trailer has started to skid by seeing it in your mirrors Any time you apply the brakes hard,

check the mirrors to make sure the trailer has not started to skid.

7.  a. Do not use the trailer hand valve in driving because of the danger of making the trailer skid. Do not use it for parking because all the air might leak out, unlocking the brakes (in trailers that do not have spring brakes).

8.  d. The purpose of the trailer air supply control is to control the tractor protection valve.

9.  b. The service line carries air, which is controlled by the foot brake or trailer hand brake. It is connected to the relay valves.

10. b. The emergency air line supplies air to the trailer air tanks and controls the emergency brakes on combination vehicles.

11. a. If there is a leak and the trailer air tank becomes empty, without spring brakes, the vehicle will have no brakes; that is why wheel chocks should be used.

12. a. Shut-off valves are used in the service and supply air lines at the back of trailers used to tow other trailers. These valves permit closing the airlines off when another trailer is not being towed.

13. a. If the trailer is too low, the tractor may strike and damage the trailer nose. If the trailer is too high, it may not couple correctly.

14. d. Make sure there is no space between the upper and lower fifth

wheel. If there is space, something is wrong (the kingpin may be on top of the closed fifth wheel jaws, and the trailer would come loose very easily).

15. a

16. c. Raise the landing gear all the way up. Never drive with landing gear only part way up, it may catch on railroad tracks or other things.

17. a. Shut off valves at the back of the last trailer should be closed. Shut off valves on trailers and dollies should be open.

18. a. To check that air flows to all the trailers, you open the emergency line shut-off valve at the rear of the last trailer; you should hear air escaping. Open the service line valve to check that service pressure goes through all the trailers. You MUST have air all the way to the back for all brakes to work.

19. C

20. b. To test the trailer emergency brakes, you should pull out the air supply control or place it in the "emergency" position. Pull gently on the trailer with the tractor to check that the trailer emergency brakes are on.

CPSIA information can be obtained
at www.ICGtesting.com
Printed in the USA
BVHW081446150321
602550BV00007B/695

9 781802 240993